*Scarcity and Survival
in Central America*

William H. Durham

Scarcity and Survival
in Central America

Ecological Origins of the Soccer War

Stanford University Press, Stanford, California

Stanford University Press
Stanford, California

© 1979 by the Board of Trustees of the
Leland Stanford Junior University

Printed in the United States of America
Cloth ISBN 0-8047-1000-7
Paper ISBN 0-8047-1154-2

Original edition 1979
Last figure below indicates year of this printing:
91   90   89   88   87

To the memory of my brother Jim

Preface

In both the academic literature and the popular press, the so-called Soccer War between El Salvador and Honduras in 1969 is cited as a classic illustration of the problems of overpopulation. The conflict has been called a "demographic war" and a veritable "population explosion." It has even been argued that the Soccer War represents in microcosm what may be in store for a world whose human population continues to increase at a rapid rate.

Despite the importance attached to the conflict as an example of population pressure, there has been no systematic attempt to evaluate the underlying assumptions of the explanation. The massive emigration of Salvadoreans to Honduras, for example, is widely conceded to have precipitated the war, but no one has demonstrated that this emigration was wholly or even chiefly a response to population pressure. Similarly, although it has been argued that the stream of Salvadoreans added significantly to Honduras's own population problems, few authors have actually assessed the impact of the immigrants at the local or national level. An evaluation of these assumptions is the goal of this study.

My analysis is perhaps best described as a case study in human ecology—broadly defined as the study of the patterns and processes of human adaptation to environments. Because the patterns and processes of human adaptation in this world are not cleanly compartmentalized, studies in human ecology are legitimately approached from any number of disciplinary perspectives, including anthropology, population biology, sociology, and demography.

This study is no exception. On the national level, I analyze census data and estimates of population size, farmland, and agricultural production using a methodology derived from demography and population biology. My purpose in these sections is to show what inferences can and cannot be drawn from aggregate data concerning the causes and effects of the Salvadorean emigration to Honduras. On the local level, I employ a methodology based on participant observation and household surveys as used in anthropology and sociology. The local-level studies provide answers to different kinds of questions than can be asked of the available aggregate data. They are an important supplement to understanding the significance of the Salvadorean migration. But as I hope to show, information from both sources is crucial to understanding the origins of the conflict between El Salvador and Honduras.

It is appropriate to make a few comments at the outset about the reliability of the national-level data used in this study. In both countries my data were compiled from official publications of the Census Bureaus and Ministries of Agriculture. These data, I believe, can be taken as reasonably accurate for several reasons. First, both countries have relatively small land areas, and each is further subdivided into more than 260 administrative and census-tract units. Logistics and scale therefore present fewer problems in the collection of national data than in other Latin American countries. Second, both countries have unusually comprehensive historical records, with estimates of population, commerce, and agriculture—in some cases yearly—dating back to 1900. El Salvador in particular had the advantage of some able early statisticians, under whose leadership the Census Bureau conducted its first extensive and systematic population census in 1892 and founded its own Department of Agricultural Statistics in 1929. Third, both countries have received international assistance with their national censuses, including some post-censal evaluation and error analysis. In one such follow-up study of Honduras's Second National Agricultural Census (Zobel 1967), the number of farms in a sample municipality was reported to have been underestimated by 7.4 percent, and the size of the farms by an average of 3.4 percent. Further, according to this study, the degree of underestimation was noticeably greater for the larger farms. As may be seen below, estimation errors like these, though relatively minor, would make my analysis a conservative appraisal of the land problems of these countries. Finally, I have tried wherever possible to incorporate additional controls and consistency checks in the data. For example, both countries have changed the census definitions of urban, rural, and economically ac-

tive population several times in the last 50 years. Fortunately, munici-
pal-level figures were available, so that I was able to recalculate these
statistics in a consistent fashion for the census years.

For the analysis itself I have relied heavily on a graphical presentation of the data. This procedure has as one advantage the simplifica-
tion and condensation of sometimes ponderous quantities of statistics.
Moreover, a graphical presentation has the advantage of permitting
less concern with absolute values than with major trends in important
variables. This technique lends itself particularly well to the analysis
of dynamics and the change of variables in a historical perspective.

The study focuses on the period from 1892 to 1971. The year 1892 is
an appropriate starting point for several reasons. First, that year saw
the first population census in El Salvador that was systematic and
thorough enough to enable a reliable estimate of the country's agricultural population. Second, it was near 1892 that El Salvador's population regained its pre-conquest level and began growing at the dramatic
rates that have continued to the present. Indeed, some authors have
argued that El Salvador has been overpopulated since that time (e.g.,
Vogt 1946). Third, the year 1892 approximately coincides with the
onset of major changes in land tenure in rural El Salvador wrought by
the Liberal Reform measures of the 1880's. And, finally, 1892 also
coincides with the beginning of large-scale commercial agriculture in
Honduras, the so-called Banana Boom, that was to have a lasting
influence on both the land tenure there and the Salvadorean immigration. The data analysis extends through 1971, which is not only the
year of the most recent census in El Salvador, but also a full two years
after the Soccer War. Although this study is primarily concerned with
population and resource dynamics preceding the conflict, I have at-
tempted to bring the reader up to date with a brief account of postwar
trends in the concluding chapter.

Many people have contributed to this study in every stage of its
development. I particularly wish to thank Kent Flannery, Brian Haz-
lett, Daniel Janzen, and Roy Rappaport for their comments and assistance as members of my doctoral committee. John Vandermeer,
who chaired the committee, has given strong support to my interest in
human ecology from the beginning, and that support has been much
appreciated. I give special thanks also to Bernard Nietschmann for his

help in the pre-fieldwork stages of this project. I would also like to express my gratitude to Peggy Barlett, Loy Bilderbach, Carlos de Sola, Kathryn Dewey, Paul Ehrlich, Galio Gurdian, Reynaldo Martorell, Elizabeth Perry, and the members of the Stanford-Berkeley Seminar on Historical Demography for their helpful comments on this research. In addition, I thank Mark Lincoln and Barbara Mnookin for their help in preparing the final manuscript. The Oxford University Press and David H. Browning have graciously permitted me to reproduce the map on p. 41; I thank them both.

Contrary to the custom of previous generations of researchers, I cannot pay homage to my wife for the patient typing of preliminary drafts of this manuscript, for that was not her role. Instead, Kathleen Foote Durham has been involved in this project from beginning to end as chief intellectual critic. I would also like to acknowledge Kathy's contributions to the fieldwork during periods of leave from her own research. In addition, she drew the maps for this publication and edited the entire text into comprehensible English.

By far the greatest debt I have incurred in the course of this study is to the people of Tenancingo and Langue, who not only welcomed me and my assistants into their homes, but willingly shared their life histories and agricultural expertise with us. Their cooperation provided invaluable insight into the causes and consequences of resource scarcity. In addition, this fieldwork would not have been possible without the support of government officials in El Salvador and Honduras. I am especially grateful to the personnel of the Ministry of Education of El Salvador and the Instituto Geográfico Nacional of Honduras for their assistance. I also thank the local authorities in the communities where I worked for their full cooperation. Many Central American friends and colleagues must remain anonymous here, but by making the study available to them I hope to repay them in part for their valuable contributions to this work.

Finally, financial support for this study came from a National Science Foundation Pre-doctoral Fellowship and from the Society of Fellows at the University of Michigan. I am deeply grateful to both institutions for that assistance.

W.H.D.

Contents

Photographs follow pages 66 and 133

Tables

Figures

*Scarcity and Survival
in Central America*

CHAPTER ONE

Introduction

On July 14, 1969, the armed forces of the Republic of El Salvador invaded the territory of the neighboring Republic of Honduras. The attack began a war that lasted only 100 hours, but left several thousand dead on both sides, turned 100,000 people into homeless and jobless refugees, destroyed half of El Salvador's oil refining and storage facilities, and paralyzed the nine-year-old Central American Common Market (Cable 1969; Fagan 1970). A cease-fire hastily arranged by the Organization of American States (OAS), coupled with a threat of rigorous economic sanctions, prompted El Salvador to withdraw its troops from Honduran territory in late July.

Because the outbreak of hostilities came just after three hotly contested soccer games in the qualifying rounds for the 1969 World Cup, the conflict was quickly labeled "the Soccer War" by foreign reporters. There were, however, at least three more important, if less obvious, issues than that name implies. For one thing, the two countries were at odds because of the effects of the 1960 Common Market Agreement on their economies. The terms of the agreement had proved to be unfortunate for the Honduran economy. Despite a favorable balance of trade outside Central America (largely through the export of primary products—bananas, meat, and lumber), Honduran imports of regional manufactured goods far surpassed the demand of other Central American countries for Honduran exports. This both hurt the country's incipient industrial sector and created a serious trade imbalance. El Salvador's economic situation was exactly the reverse. It had an unfavorable balance of trade outside the Common Market, but a very favorable balance within it, thanks to a rapid expansion of industrial exports. According to Frank T. Bachmura (1971:

286), Honduran leaders came to resent the fact that their country was effectively providing a subsidy for the industrial development of other Central American republics, particularly their neighbor to the southwest.

A second issue concerned the border between the two countries, which had remained in dispute for the 130 years of their existence as independent nations. Despite efforts as early as 1895 and 1918 to draw up demarcation treaties, El Salvador and Honduras continued to make conflicting claims to border regions, including several islands off the Pacific coast. J. A. Gerstein (1971) has linked the numerous clashes along the border in the years before the war (and after as well) directly to this problem of undefined boundaries.

A third critical issue concerned the presence in Honduras of some 300,000 Salvadorean immigrants, or roughly one of every eight persons in Honduras in 1969. In June of that year, Honduras reversed its policy of tolerating the immigration and suddenly began expelling large numbers of these Salvadoreans from their rural homesteads. This action prompted the government of El Salvador to close its borders to refugees and to file a complaint before the Inter-American Commission on Human Rights. Shortly thereafter it launched its attack on Honduras.

Because of the prominent role played by the expulsion of Salvadorean immigrants in the outbreak of the war, the third issue is widely viewed as the key issue behind the Soccer War.* In addition, it is the only issue of the three that can explain why El Salvador initiated the clash—not only was El Salvador highly favored by the Common Market, but it was already in control of most of the disputed border areas. It therefore becomes important to ask: (1) Who were these immigrants and why were they in Honduras prior to 1969? (2) Why did the Honduran government undertake its campaign to remove many of them from the countryside? (3) Why did the government of El Salvador not welcome back its countrymen but instead see their expulsion as reason to invade Honduras?

---

* Throughout the text, the term Soccer War is used simply as a shorthand reference to the 1969 conflict between El Salvador and Honduras. Of course, as this analysis will show, the conflict went far deeper than a disputed soccer match. For the record, Honduras won the first game of a best-of-three series (in Tegucigalpa, June 8, 1969) and El Salvador the second (June 15, in El Salvador). The Salvadorean team took the third game (played in Mexico City because of rising tensions, June 29).

Attempts by scholars to answer these questions have commonly focused on El Salvador's large and rapidly expanding population. Quite simply, the argument goes, the Salvadoreans moved into Honduras in search of land and jobs because they could find neither in their overpopulated homeland; and the Hondurans, who were themselves experiencing an exponential growth in population, recognized by 1969 that the immigrants were contributing to a growing shortage of their own national resources and so demanded their expulsion.

The "Population Problem"

That overpopulation should be the favored explanation of the Soccer War is not especially surprising. For years, this explanation has been given for growing problems of resource scarcity and environmental deterioration around the world by many human ecologists and other scholars. To cite but a few examples, there is Paul Ehrlich's statement (1968: 11) that "we must take action to reverse the deterioration of our environment before population pressure permanently ruins our planet"; Garrett Hardin's "lifeboat ethics" metaphor (1974a; 1974b; 1977), in which population growth causes the world's poor to "fall out" of their increasingly crowded lifeboat support systems; William Ophuls's "basic agricultural predicament" (1977: 51), in which "ignorance and the sheer pressure on resources from overpopulation" are causing land to be exploited unwisely, especially in the tropics, where in some areas "a ravenous scourge of peasants is virtually devouring the land"; and Georg Borgstrom's "food and people dilemma" (1973: 14), in which "the unquestionable fact remains that a population explosion — completely independent of economic systems — sharpens the struggle for survival."

One of the reasons for the predominant focus on overpopulation as the cause of scarcity is simply the unprecedented size and growth rate of the world's population at present. This population growth, which has been described as "the most significant terrestrial event of the past million millennia" (Ehrlich & Ehrlich 1972: 1), is often the most visible change affecting the availability of resources, whether at the international, national, or local level.

Recent theoretical work in nonhuman ecology also helps to account for the emphasis on the human "population explosion" as the cause of the world's growing food and land problems. There, resource scarcity is commonly viewed as the product of inter- and intraspecies resource competition. That competition, in turn, is assumed to be a function of changes in the population of competitors, alone or in combination with changes in the supply of resources.* Shortages therefore arise as "two (or more) animals [endeavor] to gain the same particular thing, or to gain the measure each wants from a supply of a thing, when that supply is not sufficient for both (or all)" (Milne 1961: 60). According to this view, competition is "the combined demand for resources by organisms in excess of the available supply" (Collier et al. 1973: 228).

It is true that several of these "density-dependent" models of inter- and intraspecific competition have been verified in experiments with natural populations (e.g., Eisenberg 1966; Brockelman 1969; H. Wilbur 1972) and with laboratory cultures (e.g., Vandermeer 1969). But the theory has been confirmed only in groups with little or no social structure; and in such groups, scarcity can safely be ascribed to the multiplication of competitors. It is clearly a "population problem."

Difficulties arise, however, when these simple, essentially asocial notions of competition are used to explain competition and resource scarcity in human populations. As a number of authors have pointed out, resource scarcity is not simply the result of increasing numbers of people, but may instead reflect social patterns that create unequal access to resources on a local, national, or international level (see, e.g., Meek 1971; Bahr et al. 1972; Commoner 1975). Although unequal access is sometimes recognized by those who apply theories from population biology to the analysis of human problems, a density-dependent explanation of hunger, poverty, and resource depletion automatically assumes that social factors are of negligible importance in comparison with population dynamics.

In many respects, the recent attention given to population theories of resource scarcity by both proponents and critics is simply another round in the great population debate that has been going on since at least 1798, when Thomas Malthus published his *Essay on the Principle of Population*. The history of this debate has been thoroughly reviewed elsewhere (Hutchinson 1967; Hauser 1969; Overbeek 1974; Chase 1977) and does not bear repeating here. But let us at least recall Mal-

---

* For a discussion of mathematical models of resource competition, see Appendix A.

thus's original statement of the argument. His "principle of population" is simple and straightforward:

> I think I may fairly make two postulata.
> First, that food is necessary to the existence of man.
> Secondly, that passion between the sexes is necessary and will remain nearly in its present state.
> These two laws, ever since we have had any knowledge of mankind, appear to have been fixed laws of our nature, and as we have not hitherto seen any alteration in them, we have no right to conclude that they will ever cease to be what they are now. . . .
> Assuming then my postulata as granted, I say that the power of population is indefinitely greater than the power in the earth to produce subsistence for man.
> Population when unchecked increases in a geometrical ratio. Subsistence increases only in an arithmetic ratio. A slight acquaintance with numbers will show the immensity of the first power in comparison with the second.
> By that law of our nature which makes food necessary to the life of man, the effects of these two unequal powers must be kept equal.
> This implies a strong and constantly operating check on population from the difficulty of subsistence. This difficulty must fall somewhere and must necessarily be severely felt by a large portion of mankind. (Malthus 1970: 70–71)

Malthus believed this principle to be not only the major cause of misery, poverty, and hunger throughout history, but also a force so powerful that

> no possible form of society could prevent the almost constant action of misery upon a great part of mankind, if in a state of inequality, and upon all, if all were equal. The theory on which the truth of this position depends appears to me so extremely clear that I feel at a loss to conjecture what part of it can be denied. (*Ibid.*, p. 79)

A number of modern-day authors share this enthusiasm. Among them is Georg Borgstrom, who believes that Malthus's analysis has withstood the test of time so well that his assertions are "almost axiomatic and should really be above controversy and argument" (1973: 26). Another is John Bodley, for whom "the 'green revolution,' the world food conferences, and the enormous food-aid programs are all part of the attempt to keep the two great powers, population and food production, in balance while avoiding the misery that must inevitably occur as the balance shifts in favor of population. Malthus is now being vindicated, not disproven" (1976: 88).

The Soccer War as a Test Case

Although the relationship of population growth to resource scarcity has again become one of the major topics of debate in human ecology, there have been surprisingly few careful assessments of the relative importance of population and social factors. Instead, anecdotal evidence and global generalizations have clouded the issue. Moreover, many of the aggregate data analyses that have been undertaken have a time depth of no more than ten years, and most consider only a few of the important variables.

I decided to undertake a more longitudinal, comprehensive study of one specific "population problem" in order to examine the adequacy of the prevalent theory. This study investigates the role of resource competition in the development of the conflict between El Salvador and Honduras. Looking at both population and resource dynamics in their historical context, the study analyzes the cause of land scarcity in the two countries and its consequences for the relations between them. My analysis attempts to offer a more complete ecological model for understanding resource scarcity and related social problems than is allowed by the pervasive density-dependent theory.

Let me note at the outset that I am not concerned here with the details of the war itself. The clash lasted only four days, and much of the fighting took place in remote areas where the events went unreported. Nor shall I attempt to analyze the wider political and economic issues involved in the conflict, which have been well described by other authors (see, e.g., Cable 1969; Fagan 1970; Bachmura 1971; Carías & Slutzky 1971; Jonas 1973). My aim, rather, is to examine and explain the ecological dynamics behind resource scarcity. I hope to show that these dynamics had a direct and incisive influence on the relations between the two countries.

An ecological analysis of the origins of the Soccer War is appropriate for several reasons. First, El Salvador does indeed appear to be a classic case of overpopulation. It is the most densely populated mainland country in the Western Hemisphere, and in fact is even more densely populated than India, an acknowledged standard of comparison.* Moreover, El Salvador's rate of population growth, which aver-

---

* United Nations estimates for 1976 put El Salvador's total density at 190 people per square kilometer, compared with India's 186.

aged 3.5 percent per year over the intercensal period 1961–71, is one of the highest in the world. The growing population has not only strained the country's natural resources, but is also credited with causing considerable damage to the environment—including the destruction of virtually all the indigenous natural habitats from coastal mangrove swamps to high elevation cloud forests, the extinction of more than 20 mammalian taxa since 1900, among them monkeys and porcupines (Daugherty 1969), and the accelerated erosion of an estimated 77 percent of the land area (OAS 1974: 5; see also Vogt 1946, 1948). One might reasonably expect, then, that an analysis of the causes and effects of resource scarcity in this extreme case, "one of the most environmentally devastated countries of the New World" (Eckholm 1976: 167), would contribute to our understanding of so-called population pressure in other parts of the world.

Beyond this, El Salvador and Honduras have both been identified as "food priority countries" by the United Nations on the basis of their low average incomes, projected deficits in cereal grains, and widespread nutritional deficiencies (Wortman 1976). Aggregate statistics suggest, moreover, that not only is the per-capita food supply declining in both countries, but the shortage is growing at a rapid rate (e.g., Vogt 1965; Annegers 1967). Nutritional surveys conducted by the Institute of Nutrition of Central America and Panama (INCAP 1969) demonstrate what these trends mean in human terms. They indicate that roughly 80 percent of the children under five years of age in El Salvador suffer from identifiable malnutrition (i.e., their weight-for-age ratio is more than 10 percent below normal). Nearly half of these (127,000 of 268,000) are estimated to show signs of moderate to severe malnutrition (more than 25 percent below normal weight for age). In Honduras the corresponding estimates show that 58 percent of the children under five are affected, with 41 percent of these (102,000 of 251,000) in the moderately to severely malnourished category. A recent review of the ecology of malnutrition in Central America and Mexico emphasizes that the average diet in El Salvador and Honduras is still inadequate, particularly in rural areas (May & McClellan 1972). As the authors suggest, the causes of this food shortage merit careful analysis.

Finally, the Soccer War has attracted the attention of a number of ecologists and scholars from other disciplines. In *Ecoscience: Popula-*

tion, Resources, and Environment (1977), the text widely considered the primer of human ecology, Ehrlich, Ehrlich, and Holdren draw special attention to this event in their section on population, resources, and war:

In 1969 the world saw in microcosm what may be in store: Two grossly over-populated Central American countries, El Salvador and Honduras, went to war against each other. El Salvador had an estimated population of 3.3 million, a population density of 160 per square kilometer, with a doubling time of 21 years. Honduras had a population of 2.5 million, a density of only 22 per square kilometer, and the same doubling time as El Salvador. . . .

Almost 300,000 Salvadoreans had moved into Honduras in search of land and jobs because of overpopulation and resulting unemployment at home. Friction developed among the immigrants and the Honduran natives; El Salvador accused Honduras of maltreating the Salvadoreans; and the problem escalated into a brief but nasty war. The conflict was ended by the intervention of the Organization of American States (OAS). In a precedent-shattering move, the OAS recognized demographic factors in its formula for settling the dispute—an international body acknowledged that population pressure was a root cause of war. (Ehrlich, Ehrlich, & Holdren 1977: 908, citing the *Population Bulletin*, December 1969)

Similarly, in a review of the sociological causes and consequences of population growth, Shirley Hart states that "the short war between Honduras and El Salvador in 1969 was clearly attributable to the press of population" (1972: 285). In *The Population Challenge*, Johannes Overbeek likewise concludes that the El Salvador–Honduras conflict provides empirical and logical support for the theory that "population pressure makes for hunger wars" (1976: 55–56). Further, Joel Verner, in an article on El Salvador's legislative attitude toward over-population, argues that many of the country's development problems, as well as its clash with Honduras, are "rooted in its small territorial size, high population density, and exploding population" (1975: 63). Still another analyst suggests, in a study of armaments in Third World countries, that the Soccer War will come to be known as "the first serious 'population' war of the nuclear age" (Kemp 1970: 7). These arguments in the academic literature are reflected in the press reports of the events of 1969, which repeatedly emphasized the Salvadorean "population explosion" and the differential in the population densities of the two countries (e.g., "Population Explosion: Central American Mini-War," *Time*, July 25, 1969; *New York Times*, August 4, 1969).

Relatively few authors have responded with caution to these untested population arguments. Among them, the demographer Axel Mundigo (1972) has argued that the importance attached to the role of rapid population growth in the conflict needs to be carefully reconsidered. Nazli Choucri (1974) has suggested that the population trends within the two countries merely intensified social problems and hostilities arising from other sources. And Cornell Capa and J. M. Stycos (1974) have likewise pointed to other factors behind the war, including the problems of the Central American Common Market (but see Stycos 1974 for a population argument).

More generally, a National Academy of Sciences study has cautioned against premature statements of causality, given the lack of careful studies:

There is no evidence that population growth decreases the level of political stability or increases the probability of conflict, violence, and aggressive behavior.

One reason for what may be myths about population and political pathology is that population change is ordinarily associated with socioeconomic change, and change carries with it the high likelihood of at least some disruption. . . .

Another reason is the neglect of the subject by serious scholars. . . . Clearly the only antidote to unverified hypotheses applied as guides to public policy or as sources of propaganda is to increase the sophistication of tested knowledge and to disseminate the results through public education. (National Academy of Sciences 1971: 34–35)

The El Salvador–Honduras conflict may be seen as a representative case. If we are wrong in regarding that conflict as primarily a population problem, then presumably we will need to reevaluate our understanding of other so-called population problems. In the following analysis I shall therefore reexamine the use of density-dependent models of human resource competition in the hope of shedding new light on the subject.

A Theoretical Framework for the Analysis of Resource Competition in Human Populations

For the purposes of this study, resource competition may be defined as the attempt by an individual or group of individuals to gain or maintain the use of a resource in a way that reduces the availability of that resource to other individuals or groups (see Durham 1976a). A resource, in turn, may be defined as any material substance or object used by members of a population that has the potential to increase their rates of survival or fertility, or both.*

It follows from these definitions that competition for resources in short supply can directly influence the ability of individual human beings to survive and reproduce. In this context, scarcity may be considered a measure of the extent to which an individual's survival and reproduction are limited by the availability of a given resource.

In the most general case, an individual's survival and reproduction may be limited by the availability of a given resource in a nonlinear fashion (see, e.g., Sadleir 1972). For present purposes, it is reasonable to hypothesize that the general relationship is sigmoidal, as shown in Figure 1.1A. Any number of culture-specific factors, such as social organization, competition for mates, and religious practices, may affect specific features of the curve (location, slope, etc.) for a given population and resource. However, I propose that the curves are generally S-shaped. In the figure, the ability to survive and reproduce is measured by the simple reproductive success (S_{ij}) of the individual, that is, by the number of surviving descendants of individual i after j generations. Because our concern here is with resource effects, let us assume that any scatter about the general curve due to genetically inherited differences among individuals is negligible. In other words, reproductive success in this analysis is measured not among genotypes, but among consumers of varying genetic backgrounds who experience different levels of per-capita resource availability for whatever reason. Note that at level S_{max} either some other resource or factor constrains S_{ij}, or the individual concerned has achieved the maximum physiological fertility and survivorship possible under the given conditions.

Under conditions of resource competition, a given individual or group of individuals will experience a decrease in per-capita resource availability. According to the hypothesized relationship of Figure 1.1A, this relative deprivation will reduce their ability to survive and reproduce by increasing mortality or by reducing fertility, or

---

* To prevent confusion over terminology, I use "fertility" to refer to the actual number of offspring born, in line with the preferred usage of demographers, rather than "fecundity," the term conventionally used by ecologists studying nonhuman populations.

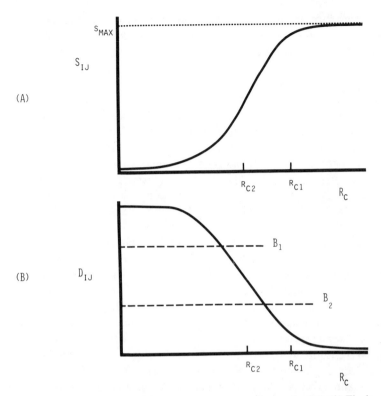

Fig. 1.1. Hypothetical relationship between resources and reproduction. (A) The hypothetical relationship between per-capita resource availability, R_c, and the ability of a consumer to survive and reproduce as measured by reproductive success, S_{ij}. S_{ij} is expected to increase monotonically with R_c until S_{max} is reached at saturation levels of resource availability. (B) Relative depression of the ability to survive and reproduce, D_{ij}, as a function of resource availability below saturation. B_1 and B_2 represent hypothetical reproductive cost levels for two behaviors that may ameliorate resource scarcity. In the model proposed, the probability of such a behavior is proportional to the difference between D_{ij} and B at a given R_c.

both. The degree of that reduction will, of course, depend on the precompetition level of resource availability. To show more clearly the effects of relative deprivation, the curve of Figure 1.1A may be inverted relative to the optimum, S_{max} (Fig. 1.1B). The inverted figure graphs the relative depression of the ability to survive and reproduce

(D_{ij}) as a function of resource availability below saturation. Figure 1.1B emphasizes that scarcity is a relative measure, and that its effects are not necessarily linear over the range of resource availability, R_c.

In combination with two additional hypotheses, this conceptualization of the relationship between resources, on the one hand, and survival and reproduction, on the other, can be used for modeling human behavioral responses to resource competition (Durham 1976a, 1976b). The first additional hypothesis is that the behaviors themselves affect the survival and reproduction chances of an individual, particularly when the behaviors require substantial amounts of time, energy, or resources, or involve the risk of injury or death. Behaviors are therefore thought to involve inherent S_{ij} "costs" to varying degrees. The kinds of behavior described as migration and aggression, for example, are believed to entail considerable costs of this kind.

The second additional hypothesis is essentially the cornerstone of contemporary thought in human ecology: whenever possible, human beings tend to behave in ways that are adaptive. (For a discussion of this hypothesis, see Richerson 1977; Durham 1979.) According to this hypothesis, a behavior characterized by high inherent costs in terms of survival and reproduction is likely to occur only when the chances are good that some compensating benefit will result. Aggressive behavior, for example, can be adaptively advantageous under certain conditions of resource competition. As long as the resource benefits of reducing the competition are greater than the costs inherent in aggressive behavior to achieve that end, aggression will be adaptive.

Figure 1.1B can be used with these hypotheses to show resource benefit thresholds for behaviors of varying costs, measured in terms of D_{ij}. To take a hypothetical case, the dotted lines labeled B_1 and B_2 in the figure represent cost levels for two given behaviors. (B_2 is less costly than B_1.) The intersection of these dotted lines with the D_{ij} curve defines critical levels of per-capita resource availability. When the action of competitors reduces access to resources below their respective critical levels, B_1 and B_2 are rendered adaptively advantageous. (As shown in the figure, B_2 has a lower critical level than B_1.) At resource availabilities below these critical levels, the probability (or frequency) of the occurrence of a behavior is expected to increase in proportion to the difference between D_{ij} and the behavior's cost level.

Although it is not the purpose of this study to provide a general elaboration and test of these underlying hypotheses (see, on this point, Durham 1976b, 1979), human migration is here treated as a behavioral response to resource scarcity. A key proposition is that the Salvadoreans emigrated to Honduras in response to resource scarcity. This will be tested by relating the frequency of migration to an indicator of D_{ij} (namely, child mortality) at different levels of resource availability.

Returning now to the population level, we can use Figure 1.1B as a framework for analyzing competition-related resource scarcity within a human population. Consider first a hypothetical population (N), which is distributed with respect to per-capita resource availability as shown by the solid line in Figure 1.2A. (A narrow, bell-shaped distribution is assumed only for purposes of clarity; other initial distributions could be substituted.) By superimposing the D_{ij} curve from Figure 1.1B along the same R_c axis, it can be seen that the average per-capita resource availability in the population ($\overline{R}_{c1}$), is associated with only a small reproduction-survival depression, A, compared with optimal conditions. Within the population some individuals experience D_{ij} values greater than A, and others experience D_{ij} values less than A.

In principle there are three ways in which competition may reduce resource availability to individuals in N (see Appendix A; Birch 1957). First, when the distribution of the population is constant, growing numbers of consumers relative to the total available resources may result in an increase of what may be called absolute scarcity. Figure 1.2B illustrates this "Malthusian model" of resource scarcity. All members of the population experience a lower per-capita resource availability in (B) than in (A). In fact, the change in average resource availability from $\overline{R}_{c1}$ to $\overline{R}_{c2}$ is a good measure of the decrease in resource availability experienced by every individual in the population (assuming a negligible amount of internal social mobility). Resource scarcity under these conditions is a density-dependent phenomenon. Our knowledge of population growth and resource dynamics is sufficient here to predict decreases in resource availability. These changes can be adequately described by conventional ecological theories of resource competition.

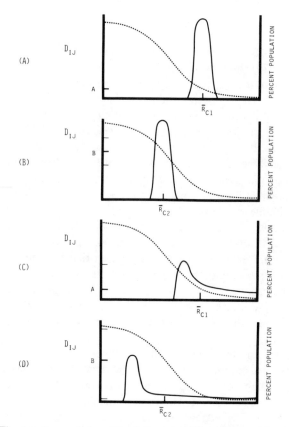

Fig. 1.2. Conceptual models of the causes of resource scarcity. (A) Precompetitive conditions in a population with a fairly even distribution of resources. The population distribution (solid curve) measured at right is juxtaposed with the relative depression curve (dotted) of Figure 1.1B. The average resource availability shown here, $\overline{R}_{c1}$, is associated with an average depression value of A. (B) The Malthusian model of resource scarcity. Population growth relative to the total resource base lowers the average per-capita availability to $\overline{R}_{c2}$. Density-dependent resource scarcity affects all members of the population, although some may be more affected than others. (C) The distribution model of resource scarcity. Resource competition within a population creates depression effects among some members, even though the average resource available remains $\overline{R}_{c1}$ as in (A). (D) The combination model of resource scarcity. Both population growth and distributional dynamics affect access to resources within the population. Their separate effects are confounded in the graph but can be factored out if information on earlier periods is available. The light ticks on the Y-axes of (B), (C), and (D) indicate the range of the depression effects within the populations.

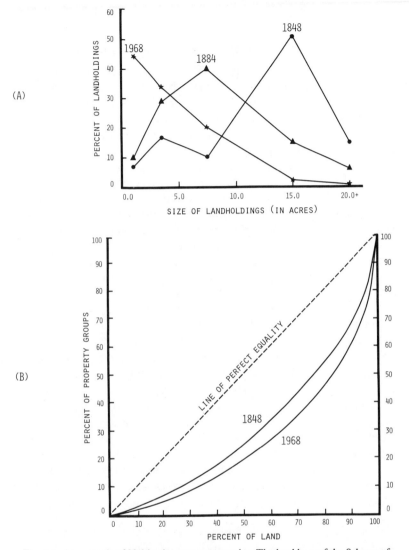

Fig. 1.3. An example of Malthusian resource scarcity: The land base of the Sahotas of Vilyatpur, India. (A) Changes in the ownership of land among Sahota property groups in 1848, 1884, and 1968. The figure shows the percentage of all landholdings by year in five size categories. The average size of all holdings was 13.1 acres in 1848, 7.6 acres in 1884, and 3.7 acres in 1968. The progressive shift in the curves from right to left on the resource availability axis (arrow) corresponds to the shift between Figures 1.2A and 1.2B in the theoretical model described. (B) Changes in the distribution of land among property groups between 1848 and 1968. The figure shows modified Lorenz curves, one for each year, depicting the cumulative percentage of all owned lands, beginning with the largest size category of 20+ acres. The plot confirms that changes between 1848 and 1968 in the distribution of land within the landholding population are relatively insignificant (compare, e.g., Fig. 2.14). The data for the intermediate years fall generally between the two curves shown here. SOURCE: Kessinger 1974: 114.

Second, changes in the distribution of a resource within a population may result in relative shortages for particular individuals or sub-populations. This "distribution model" of resource scarcity is shown in Figure 1.2C, where the average per-capita resource availability remains at $\bar{R}_{c1}$, as in Figure 1.2A, either because population growth is negligible or because it is counterbalanced by resource dynamics. Resource scarcity is therefore not density-dependent. What changes is the distribution of access to the resource through competition within the population. As shown in the figure, the average availability of the resource does not reflect the growing scarcity experienced by individuals at the lower end of the distribution. These members of the population experience considerable survival and reproduction depression, which is masked by a low $D_{ij} = A$ for the average R_c. Competitive dynamics of this kind are ignored by conventional ecological theories of resource competition. In theory, however, the distribution of resources may vary through time in human populations, and there is abundant empirical evidence that it does so (see, e.g., J. Davis 1973: Chapter 7; and example below).

Figure 1.2D illustrates the third or "combination model," where both population and distribution factors contribute to resource scarcity. As shown in the figure, the average availability of the resource, $\bar{R}_{c2}$, although lower here, still does not represent the increasingly wide range of conditions experienced by individuals in the population. The depression $(D_{ij} = B)$ for the average R_c does not accurately reflect the effects of scarcity. Here again, population growth is an inadequate explanation of resource competition within the population. Some individuals are protected from the effects of population growth because of favorable distributional changes, whereas others suffer resource losses from distributional dynamics compounded with population growth.

Some examples from the anthropological literature may help to illustrate the distinctions between these causes of resource scarcity. Tom Kessinger's study of landownership changes in a rural Punjabi village, Vilyatpur, closely conforms to the assumptions and dynamics of the Malthusian model. Using British tax records, he has shown that between 1848 and 1968 the "per-capita decline in agricultural land and the amount of land owned by individual property groups was a direct consequence of the growth of Vilyatpur's population"

(1974: 113). This inference is strongest for the case of the Sahota landowning subcaste. In the period studied, the number of Sahota "property groups" (households with joint property rights) increased from 41 to 146 as a result of population growth. The average size of their holdings meanwhile decreased from 13.1 acres to 3.7 acres. As shown in Figure 1.3A, this land was not evenly distributed among the groups. However, the figure suggests that the distribution itself did not change drastically over the years; rather, it appears to have simply shifted left on the resource-availability axis as the number of property groups increased. This relatively constant distribution is confirmed by Figure 1.3B, which shows a modified Lorenz curve for the land-ownership data from Kessinger's study. Because both axes are measured in percentages, the plot shows only distributional changes and ignores shifts in the size of farm units. The distributional change is relatively insignificant in comparison with the shift shown in (A). Thus the data nicely support Kessinger's conclusion that the Sahota property groups experienced increasing land scarcity as a direct consequence of their population growth. The case must be considered rather special, however, because of the caste structure of the society, and because in the period studied, the Sahota subcaste was the only one of the 12 in the village to own land. (In 1968 it accounted for 45 percent of the total village population.)

A 1977 paper by Thomas Love on the Almond Valley near Sacramento, California, illustrates how distributional changes can generate resource scarcity. In that valley the distribution of farmland has shifted drastically since the late 1950's, owing to an influx of people from urban areas seeking retirement farms. This shift, described by Love as "competitive displacement," began at a time when small full-time farmers were under economic pressure to expand their landholdings in order to achieve greater economies of scale. Many of the full-timers were unable to compete for land with the retirement farmers, whose outside income enabled them to pay higher prices. As a result, the full-time farmers "have been literally 'losing ground' to 'retirement' farms" (p. 36). The competition reportedly forced some farmers to enlarge their holdings and many others to sell out. As the model in Figure 1.2C would predict, the total number of farms has not increased significantly, but the urban influx has changed the distribution of land among full-time farms in two ways (see Love's schematic plots of distributional changes, p. 38). First, the proportion of medium-sized, full-time farmers—those able to expand despite high costs—has increased modestly, and second, the proportion of full-time farmers with little or no land of their own has increased dramatically. The land available to full-time farmers approximates the distributional change of Figure 1.2C, with the exception that the left end of the distribution curve here corresponds to $R_c = 0$.

I have briefly discussed these two cases to illustrate some of the distinctions between the conceptual models of resource scarcity presented in Figure 1.2. Additional examples, including the combination model, will be discussed in the analysis of resource scarcity in El Salvador and Honduras. I should mention, however, that scarcity under the conditions of Figure 1.2D may well be the result of an interaction between population growth and resource distribution. Consider, for example, a social system that institutionally perpetuates unequal access to a resource and thereby allows a few families to maintain high values of R_c over long periods of time. If the total resource supply does not proportionately increase in time, the growth of this population will cause resource scarcity. In contrast to the situation in Figure 1.2B, however, population growth here will have a multiplying effect on the distribution. The resources available to the poor will diminish at a rate that exceeds the decreases in average resource availability. The uncritical observer of this process may fail to notice that population growth exacerbates resource scarcity mostly or only among the poor.

In addition to these conceptual distinctions, Figure 1.2 also suggests ways in which the causes of resource scarcity in a population may be inferred from information on the changes of resource availability over time. In theory, even if simultaneous population and distribution dynamics influence access to resources, as in Figure 1.2D, the relative effects of the two factors can still be determined. One simply needs to compare the changes over time in per-capita resource availability by strata within the distribution. Strata whose per-capita average decreases more or faster than the overall average are experiencing a distributional dynamic in addition to population growth. The relative importance of the two factors can then be inferred by comparing the magnitude of the strata decrease with the average decrease. This technique for analyzing the causes of resource scarcity is used in Chapter Two in the discussion of El Salvador's land resources.

It should be noted that the variable D_{ij} in these models of resource scarcity is the ecological synonym for what is commonly called population pressure. As shown in these figures, however, changes in this "pressure" can readily be generated by more than population dynamics. Depending both on the initial distribution of resources and on changes in that distribution over time, population pressure may become great for some members of a population even where aggregate scarcity is not a major problem. In such a situation, the reasoning behind Figure 1.1B would lead one to expect members of the population to respond differently to growing resource scarcity.

In a similar fashion, Ray Kelly (1968) and Marshall Sahlins (1972) have argued that the causes of scarcity and the responses to it in human populations generally arise from cultural variables, as well as from population and resource dynamics. These cultural variables commonly affect resource distribution:

> In any given cultural formation, "pressure on land" is not in the first instance a function of technology and resources, but rather of the producer's *access* to *sufficient* means of livelihood. The latter is clearly a specification of the cultural system—relations of production and property, rules of land tenure, relations between local groups, and so forth. Except in the theoretically improbable case in which the customary rules of access and labor are consistent with optimum exploitation of land, a society may experience "population pressure" of various kinds at global densities below its technical capacity of production. . . . Moreover, how this pressure is organizationally experienced, the level of social order to which it is communicated, *as well as the character of the response*, also depend on the institutions in place. . . . Hence both the definition of population pressure and its social effects pass by way of the existing structure. (Sahlins 1972: 49)

In theoretical terms, then, one might well expect the cases in which population growth adequately explains resource scarcity to be relatively rare. As shown in Appendix A, an *a priori* assumption of the insignificance of distributional dynamics is often weakest in large and growing populations. As Sahlins concludes, "Any explanation of historical events or developments, such as warfare or the origin of the state, that ignores this [existing institutional] structure is theoretically suspect" (1972: 49).

In the following chapters, I attempt to relate the theoretical framework of Figures 1.1 and 1.2 to the resource competition in and between El Salvador and Honduras. A thorough analysis of the population and resource dynamics behind the Soccer War must attempt to answer three major questions: (1) What actually caused the out-migration of the estimated 300,000 Salvadoreans to Honduras? (2) What was the impact in Honduras of this growing immigrant population? (3) How was that impact related to the development of the conflict? The first question is discussed in the next two chapters. Identifying the reasons for the Salvadorean migration to Honduras is crucial not only for interpreting the history of the conflict, but also for obtaining a clearer understanding of the problems of so-called population pressure in El Salvador. Chapter Two analyzes the historical causes of resource scarcity in El Salvador at a national level and compares the relative contributions of population growth and distributional dynamics to the increasing scarcity of farmland there. In Chapter Three I then relate resource scarcity to Salvadorean peasant migration, based on the results of a local survey study of a small rural community of El Salvador.

I address the second and third questions in Chapters Four and Five. Chapter Four compares Honduras's general agricultural situation with El Salvador's, examines the dynamics of resource competition in Honduras, and evaluates the potential of the immigrants for contributing to mounting land scarcity in that country. In Chapter Five I use the data from a second local study to clarify the nature and extent of the Salvadorean influence in Honduras. Finally, in Chapter Six I attempt to reinterpret the causes of the Soccer War and discuss some of the implications of this study for our understanding of other "population problems."

CHAPTER TWO

The Causes of Resource Scarcity in El Salvador

El Salvador is frequently cited as a country whose population has simply outgrown its food supply. Although population growth may indeed contribute to the country's shortages of food and other resources, our preceding discussion suggests that other factors may well be involved. Using the theoretical framework developed in the last chapter, let us now compare the Malthusian and non-Malthusian causes of resource scarcity in El Salvador.

The Malthusian Model

At first glance, El Salvador does appear to provide an excellent argument for the Malthusian model of resource scarcity. To begin with, there are clear indications of a "geometrical tendency" in the country's population growth. As shown in Figure 2.1, it took almost 400 years for the population to recover from the ravages of the Spanish conquest, which saw the rapid decimation of the Indian population through warfare, epidemics, and the slave trade. By the early 1900's, however, exponential increase—or what William Vogt (1948) calls "El Salvador's parabola of misery"—was already well in evidence. The average annual growth rate of the population has also tended to increase over time, as shown in Table 2.1. By the time of the Soccer War, that rate had reached a record 3.49 percent.

From at least the late 1800's to 1971, then, the exponential growth curve of the population clearly conforms to the Malthusian model. The evidence also points to an increasingly serious problem of food supply as the population has expanded. In Figure 2.2, which compares El Salvador's population growth and food production from 1932

T A B L E 2.1　*Population Growth of El Salvador, 1570–1971*

Year	Estimated population on July 1	Average annual growth rate in the interval
1570	77,000	0.31%
1778	146,700	1.07
1807	200,000	1.42
1855	394,000	1.50
1878	554,800	1.71
1892	703,500	1.90
1930	1,436,900	1.30[a]
1950	1,859,500	2.81
1961	2,523,200	3.49
1971	3,555,800	

SOURCE: Interpolations based on estimates compiled by Daugherty 1969 and on census data from ESDGEC 1942, 1953, 1965, 1974a.

[a] The growth rate for this interval reflects the demographic consequences of a peasant rebellion in 1932, in which an estimated 17,000 people were killed (Torres 1962: 10).

to 1971, we see the population increasing at an accelerating rate through the period, while food production stagnates in the 1950's and then falls seriously behind. The data also indicate some faltering of production in the 1930's and 1940's (possibly compounded with errors in early production estimates), but these shortages, confirmed by Bourne et al. 1974, lasted only a few years.

Figure 2.2 thus provides evidence for a persistent shortfall in the food supply beginning in the mid-1950's and continuing through at least 1971. Before that, although production varied considerably, the food supply apparently increased at a rate sufficient to compensate for the increase in population. This inference is strengthened by the early production estimates of Antonio Gutiérrez y Ulloa (1807). Comparing his figures with the average production figures for the 1930's, we find an 850 percent increase in maize, a 750 percent increase in beans, and a huge 7,300 percent increase in rice. In the meantime, the population increased only 670 percent. Thus, El Salvador's post-1950 problems do look very much like a Malthusian crisis, a persistent food scarcity (the first in the country's history, as far as we know from the written record) caused by an imbalance between the "power of population" and the "power in the earth to produce subsistence."

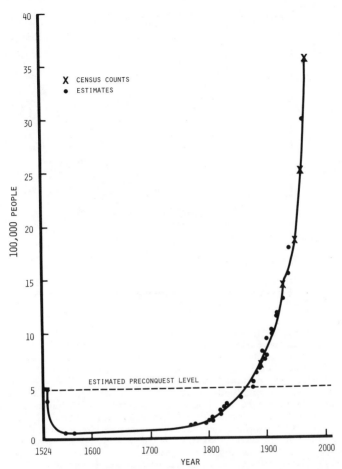

Fig. 2.1. Population growth of El Salvador, 1524–1971. Estimates before 1839 are based on colonial records and Indian tribute payments. SOURCE: Menjivar 1962; Daugherty 1969; Denevan 1976; Barón Castro 1978.

The result of these trends has been an increased aggregate "difficulty of subsistence" (in Malthus's terms), as shown in Figure 2.3. This figure shows the relationship between the per-capita production of basic food crops for 1932–71 and the average per-capita production for 1932–50 of 3.46 *quintales* (1 quintal = 45.4 kg = 100 pounds). The figure does not tell the whole story, however. It shows what has happened quantitatively to the food supply, but it does not show that it has also deteriorated qualitatively. As a number of authors have commented, El Salvador is the only Latin American country in which

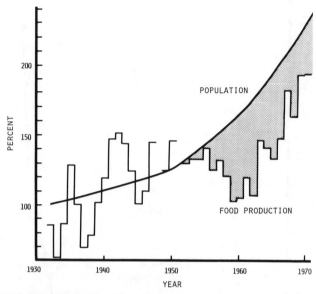

Fig. 2.2. Population growth and food production in El Salvador, 1932–1971. Population percentages were calculated relative to base year 1932, using July 1 interpolations between the census totals of 1930, 1950, 1961, and 1971. The 1932 figure was adjusted to take into account an estimated 17,000 deaths from a peasant rebellion that year. Food increases are based on official yearly production estimates for the four basic food crops: maize *(Zea mays)*, beans *(Phaseolus vulgaris)*, rice *(Oryza sativa)*, and sorghum *(Sorghum vulgare)*. To estimate the total annual food production, yearly kilogram totals were summed for all four crops and then converted to percentages of the 1932–50 average (use of an average baseline figure was necessary because of high variability in early production figures). SOURCES: ESDGEC 1942, 1953, 1965, 1974a; *Anuario*, 1901–76; ESMAG, *Anuario de estadísticas agropecuarias*, 1970–75, *Anuario de prognósticos*, 1963–70; *Indicadores*, 1963–75. Estimates from these sources were tabulated and compared for each year available. Where discrepancies existed, I used the figures most consistent with the five-year trends on either side of the discrepancy.

sorghum has become an important human food as well as a livestock feed. A crop that grows comparatively well on steep slopes and depleted soils, its production increased more rapidly than maize between 1932 and 1971. In many rural areas sorghum tortillas have replaced maize tortillas as the population's daily staple.

Other studies of production trends in the 1950's and 1960's confirm this picture of per-capita deficits. For example, Vogt et al. (1967: 17), using U.S. Department of Agriculture indexes for El Salvador for

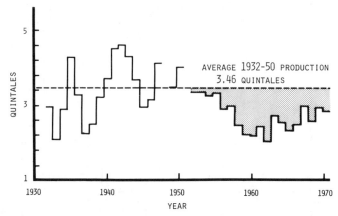

Fig. 2.3. Per-capita production of basic food crops in El Salvador, 1932–1971. The shaded area suggests an increased aggregate "difficulty of subsistence" (after Malthus). SOURCE: Same as Fig. 2.2.

1959–65, found that per-capita food production reached only 80–90 percent of the 1953–55 average in that period (see also Martínez Cuestras 1965; Annegers 1967). Similarly, according to Ayala 1968, in the years 1950–66 per-capita production fell off in all but three of the country's 14 major food products: sugar (conventionally considered an export crop because the bulk of production is not consumed domestically), vegetable oils (a by-product of another major export crop, cotton), and fish (not cultivated). Among the products whose per-capita production declined (including beef, poultry, eggs, milk, and grains), two—beans and pork—decreased not only relatively, but absolutely.

El Salvador's reliance on food imports in the 1950's and 1960's lends further support to the case for a growing Malthusian crisis. As shown in Figure 2.4, the country imported increasing quantities of basic food crops from 1950 to 1966, apparently in response to a growing scarcity of food caused by the burgeoning of the population. (The reason for the post-1966 decline in imports will be considered below.)

What all these data indicate, according to conventional interpretations, is that El Salvador is losing the Malthusian "race between population and food supply" (T. Smith 1976). As the Environmental Fund has put it, in a statement issued in 1976 and endorsed by

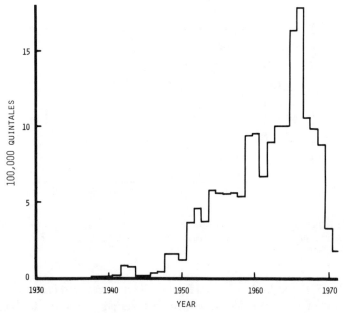

Fig. 2.4. Imports of basic food crops by El Salvador, 1932–1971. Total imports of maize, rice, beans, and sorghum by calendar year were converted to two-year sliding averages to enable comparison with production figures published by the agricultural year (May 1– April 30). SOURCE: *Anuario*, 1932–75.

Zbigniew Brzezinski, Paul Ehrlich, Garrett Hardin, Philip Hauser, and William Paddock: "The problem is too many people. The food shortage is simply evidence of the problem. . . . Some nations are now on the brink of famine because their populations have grown beyond the carrying capacity of their lands. Population growth has pushed the peoples of Africa, Asia, and Latin America onto lands which are only marginally suitable for agriculture" (p. 28).

Again El Salvador seems to be an excellent case in support of their point, since population growth appears not only to have resulted in a food shortage, but also to have led to the expansion of agriculture beyond the "carrying capacity" of the land. One often-cited example is the rapid deforestation of the country as the population has swelled. In 1807 the estimated forest cover was 60–70 percent of the total surface area; by 1946 the figure had dropped to a mere 8.3 percent (Bourne et al. 1947). As early as 1916, in fact, a publicity bureau sought to attract visitors to the country by claiming that "the land-scape presents to the traveller a scene similar to a vast checkerboard where the various products of the fertile land may be admired; from the highest peaks to the beautiful valleys and plains, Salvador presents a view that reminds us of a large and well-kept garden, with every available piece of land, even at the highest levels, being under cultivation" (cited in D. Browning 1971: 216). In 1946 it was "not uncommon to observe hillsides as steep as 100 percent (45 degrees) and more, that have been stripped of every vestige of native vegetation and planted to corn and other annually cultivated crops" (Bourne et al. 1947: 99).

Nevertheless, in the next 20 years the area under cultivation in El Salvador continued to expand. Between 1944 and 1961, it increased from 20.4 percent to 29.8 percent of the country's total surface area of 21,041 square kilometers (Bourne et al. 1947: 9; ESDGEC 1967: 70). Moreover, the agricultural census of 1961 revealed that a full 75.2 percent of that total area had been absorbed by farms. According to the Economic Commission for Latin America, this is the highest utilization figure for all of Central America (CEPAL 1971: 5). By 1969 Howard Daugherty was led to conclude (p. 185) that "the area devoted to subsistence crops has virtually reached its absolute maximum and may actually be expected to decline in the near future. Food crops are currently being cultivated on slopes which cannot withstand permanent cultivation. The productivity of such land, already marginal, will be destroyed within a few years."

Because the expansion of agriculture has generally paralleled the increase in population, population pressure is seen as the cause of the deforestation, hillside cultivation, soil erosion, and habitat destruction that have been visible in El Salvador for many years (compare Croat 1972 on Panama). According to this viewpoint, environmental degradation occurs simply because of the need to expand the food supply to meet the demands of an ever-growing population. In a real Malthusian crisis of this kind, good fertile land would be heavily used and very scarce, and even poor land and thin soils would become overutilized as the physical limits to expansion are approached. Ultimately, of course, the continued growth of the population would reduce the per-capita availability of land for food production, and Malthusian dynamics would then result in a severe land shortage.

Once again the data from El Salvador appear consistent with this interpretation. Figure 2.5 shows the per-capita amount of farmland used annually from 1932 to 1971 for the production of basic food crops. Again there is some variation in the 1930's and 1940's, but generally speaking, there is no consistent trend up or down in those decades. This "plateau" indicates that the expansion of the land area cultivated in food crops kept pace with population growth until the mid-1950's. Then, at roughly the same time as the start of the food crisis suggested by Figure 2.2, food cropland appears to have reached the limit of its growth. Beginning about 1955, the continuing increase in population seems to have caused a steady decrease in the per-capita land base for food crops. This suggests an increasingly intense density-dependent competition over land for food, or "subsistence" crops. It thus seems reasonable to impute both the shortage of food and the shortage of farmland to the "principle of population."

In a country as dependent on agriculture as El Salvador, population pressure of the magnitude suggested by Figure 2.5 would be a serious and unremitting problem for several reasons. First, it would be a major threat to the national economy. A full 25 percent to 35 percent of El Salvador's annual gross national product in the 1950's and 1960's came from agriculture (*Indicadores* 1964, 1970; see also Loenholdt

T A B L E 2.2   *Characteristics of the Population of El Salvador, 1892–1971*

Year	Censused population	Rural population[a]		Economically active population	
		Percent of total population	Percent agriculturally active	Percent of total population	Percent agriculturally active
1892	703,500	80.00%	29.38%[b]	31.23%[c]	75.27%[b]
1930	1,434,361	78.73	29.38[d]	30.73[d]	75.27[d]
1950	1,855,917	74.25	29.95	35.21	63.15
1961	2,510,984	70.35	27.52	32.14	60.24
1971	3,554,648	66.45	26.76	32.82	54.18

SOURCE: Barberena 1892; ESDGEC 1942, 1953, 1965, 1974a, 1977.

[a] Recalculated from census information using 2,500 or more inhabitants as the criterion for urban except for the census year 1892, when the rural population was assumed to be 80% of the total.

[b] 1930 figures used as a conservative estimate for 1892 percentages.

[c] Estimate derived from other assumptions for 1892.

[d] Calculated from 1930 census information on occupational categories in order to be consistent with later census definitions. The agriculturally active population figure combines the census categories of *agricultores* and *jornaleros*. The total economically active population consists of all gainfully employed males and females.

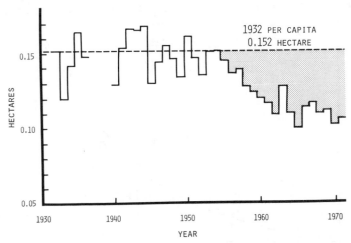

Fig. 2.5. Per-capita farmland in basic food crops in El Salvador, 1932–1971. The figure double counts areas cultivated more than once in a given year. SOURCE: Same as Fig. 2.2.

1953; Nathan & Associates 1969). Any limit to growth in this important sector would inevitably put a damper on economic growth even with real advances in other sectors (see Royer 1966; Mayorga Quirós 1974). Second, it would threaten the survival (and/or reproduction) of a large portion of the population. Not only was El Salvador's population still predominantly rural in 1971 (despite proportional decreases; see Table 2.2), but roughly 60 percent of the country's economically active population, or some 632,000 people, depended on agriculture for the sustenance of themselves and their families. Finally, *if* the scarcity of land were both (1) the result of the Malthusian population–resource dynamics shown above and (2) the principal cause of the Salvadorean migration to Honduras (and hence of the "friction" between the Hondurans and Salvadoreans), then the Soccer War itself would quite properly have been part of the country's more general "population problem."

In the remainder of this chapter we will look more closely at the validity of assertion (1) as an explanation of resource scarcity in El Salvador and of the conflict with Honduras. Assertion (2) will be considered in Chapter Three.

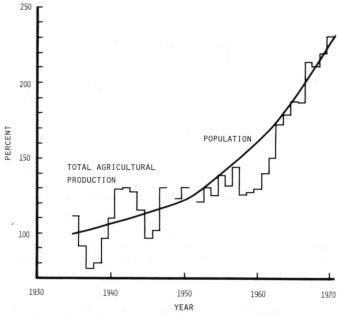

Fig. 2.6. Population growth and total agricultural production in El Salvador, 1935–1971. Yearly kilogram production totals were summed for maize, rice, beans, sorghum, coffee, cotton, and export sugar, and then converted to percentages of the 1935–50 average. The plot begins at 1935 instead of 1932 because earlier yearly production figures for cotton are not available. SOURCE: Same as Fig. 2.2.

Non-Malthusian Causes of Resource Scarcity

The Competitive Allocation of Farmland

A closer look at the patterns of food production and land use in El Salvador calls into question a simple Malthusian interpretation of food and land shortages. To begin with, when we compare the production figures for all principal crops (food crops plus exports) with the population increases for the period 1935–71 (Fig. 2.6), we see that total agricultural production has stayed pretty much abreast of population growth. This finding has two important implications. First, it suggests that the population–food production imbalance that developed in the 1950's and 1960's was not simply the result of agricultural expansion to some physical limit. That total production kept pace while the food supply did not clearly implies that land-use practices and

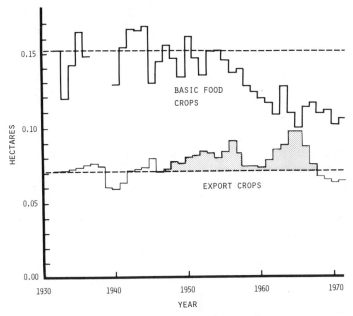

Fig. 2.7. Per-capita farmland in basic food crops (maize, rice, beans, and sorghum) and in export crops (coffee, cotton, and export sugar) in El Salvador, 1932–1971. The export crop areas are not double counted, as the food crop areas are (see Fig. 2.5), and the figure therefore exaggerates the separation of the two curves. SOURCE: Same as Fig. 2.2.

production priorities were factors in the imbalance. Second, it suggests that large increases in export production were realized in the face of growing food shortages—large enough in fact to compensate statistically for the food shortages themselves.

Further analysis of the time-series data on land use reveals a major reason why the food harvest lagged despite growing total production: food crops have consistently lost out to more profitable export crops in the competition for land. Figure 2.7 compares the per-capita land utilization figures for El Salvador's principal food and export crops from 1932 to 1971.* The meaning of the curve we see there is clear:

---

* The figure does not show the area in cattle pasture because yearly totals are not available. Census data (ESDGEC 1954, 1967, 1974b) and Annegers 1967, however, suggest a pattern equivalent to the food-crop curve shown here. Cattle are produced primarily for domestic consumption.

even in the face of exponential population growth, the proportion of per-capita land dedicated to export crops grew steadily, to reach an all-time high during the peak "food crisis" years. By the 1960's export crops accounted for an average of 41.9 percent of the total area cultivated in major crops. The allocation of substantial amounts of land to the cultivation of export crops thus emerges as an important cause of land pressure and food scarcity.

The expansion of cotton production illustrates the point nicely. Cotton is now widely grown in El Salvador's humid Pacific lowlands, an area that remained largely undeveloped through World War II because of endemic malaria. Thanks to malaria control, the completion of a littoral highway through the region, and a favorable world market, cotton expanded rapidly as a commercial crop between 1935, when 1,144 hectares were planted, and 1965, with 110,792 hectares (*Anuario* 1936: 88; CEPAL 1971: 28). This expansion corresponded, partly by coincidence, with the decades of El Salvador's most rapid population growth and presumably the most rapid growth in the demand for food. Several lines of evidence suggest that the expansion of cotton directly absorbed thousands of hectares suitable for, and needed for, the production of basic food crops. First, there is a close correlation between the expansion of cotton acreage and the importation of those crops. This is shown clearly in Figure 2.8, which compares the yearly totals of land area licensed for cotton production with yearly maize import totals in two-year sliding averages. The correlation, as shown, was strengthened by the "cotton crash" of 1965–67, when in the course of two years a white fly epidemic, an unfavorable world market, and widespread soil exhaustion combined to reduce the cotton harvest by 52.4 percent and the area licensed by 43.8 percent. By 1967 maize imports had dropped almost as much, to 44.4 percent below the 1965 level.*

A government study in 1966 of the reduced cotton acreage confirms that the relationship shown in Figure 2.8 is not a spurious correlation (Aguilar Girón 1967). Of 29,482 hectares taken out of cotton cultivation that year, 14,039 hectares, or more than 47.6 percent, were immediately turned to maize the next growing season. The conversion to

---

* The appearance of a peak in the maize imports in 1966 after the initial decline in cotton acreage is an artifact of the use of two-year sliding averages. The actual peak in imports was reached during the calendar year 1965.

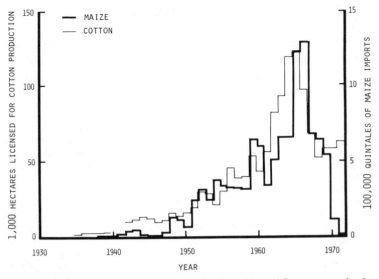

Fig. 2.8. Correlation between yearly totals of land area licensed for cotton production and maize imports in El Salvador, 1930–1971. Because the calendar year is used for import figures and the agricultural year for licensing acreages, official annual import figures have been converted to two-year sliding averages. SOURCE: Cotton, Cooperativa Algodonera Salvadoreña 1972. Maize imports, *Anuario*, 1940–52; ESMAG, *Anuario de estadísticas agropecuarias*, 1970–75, *Anuario de prognósticos*, 1963–70.

food cropland totals 57.4 percent when beans, rice, and sorghum are also counted. Another 30.5 percent of the former cotton lands were turned into pasture. Although the transformation of export cropland to food cropland was not 100 percent, that change did partially alleviate earlier production deficits (see Figs. 2.2 and 2.3). National maize production, for example, grew by 247,000 quintales between 1965 and 1966 and by a whopping 1,368,000 quintales between 1966 and 1967. Although the cotton industry was widely praised during its boom years for diversifying El Salvador's export agriculture, it is evident that the expansion contributed significantly to the stagnation of food-crop production. (On this point, see R. Smith 1965; Welton 1967; Annegers 1967.)

What is more, cotton is not even the most important export-crop competitor of the food crops. By all evidence, coffee has displaced even larger areas of corn, rice, and beans in its rapid expansion since

1850. Although statistics are lacking for most of the period, Everett Wilson has provided two graphic eyewitness accounts from the late 1920's deploring the wholesale conversion of the volcanic highlands of the southwest (mainly in southern Santa Ana and Sonsonate; see Fig. 2.9) from traditional Indian *milpas* (subsistence plots) and forest to coffee plantations:

> The conquest of territory by the coffee industry is alarming. It has already occupied all the high ground and is now descending to the valleys, displacing maize, rice, and beans. It goes in the manner of the conquistador, spreading hunger and misery, reducing the former proprietors to the worst conditions—woe to those who sell out! (*Patria*, Dec. 22, 1928, cited in Wilson 1970: 122).

> Now there is nothing but coffee. In the great hacienda named California that covers the flanks of the volcano *Alegría*, where I visited last year, I did not find a single fruit tree. On that *finca* [farm] that extends for many *caballerías* [one caballería = 45 hectares], there were formerly a hundred or more properties planted in maize, rice, beans, and fruit. Now there is nothing but coffee in the highlands, and pasture in the lowlands, which go on displacing the forests and the milpas. (*Patria*, Oct. 20, 1928, cited in *ibid.*, p. 123)

Because coffee requires fertile soils at an elevation of more than 500 meters, most of this expansion took place in the areas of densest rural settlement and traditional subsistence agriculture. We may reasonably assume, therefore, that the growth of coffee exports reflects the rate at which foodland was converted to coffee. As shown by David Luna (1971: 202–3) and Ciro Cardoso (1975), coffee exports increased dramatically between 1866 and 1915, a period in which their share of the value of the country's exports climbed from 10 percent to 85 percent. (On the expansion of coffee, see Cuenca 1962; Cardoso 1973; see also Seligson 1974 and 1975 for the description of a similar process in Costa Rica.)

This dramatic expansion in the cultivation of coffee for the external market is sometimes ignored by those who claim that the destruction of El Salvador's forest cover (to go back to our earlier example) is the result of population growth. It is true that great numbers of peasants migrated into the country's forested northern departments in the nineteenth century. Between 1770 and 1892, for instance, the population of Chalatenango grew by an average of 1.90 percent per year and that of Cabañas by 2.49 percent per year. This compares with a national annual average in that period of only 1.38 percent (Barberena 1892: 35; Barón Castro 1978: 233). But considering that thousands of

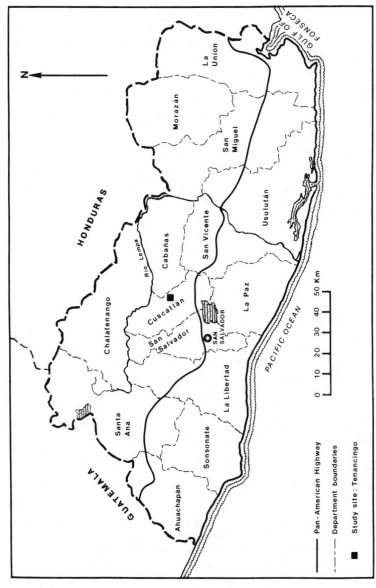

Fig. 2.9. The Republic of El Salvador. The Rio Lempa demarcates the southern border of the department of Chalatenango and the eastern borders of the departments of Cabañas and San Vincente.

peasants were displaced by the expansion of coffee, there is little justi-fication for saying that "during the 1800's . . . increasing *population pressure* resulted in a continual movement upslope of subsistence agri-culturalists and a significant movement into the mountain areas" (Daugherty 1969: 138; emphasis mine). The spread of coffee in other areas also played a major role in the peasants' exploitation of the mountain regions.

Another consequence of the coffee boom has been documented by Wilson. As with cotton, the coffee expansion produced a temporary shortage of basic food crops, which in turn led to sharply increased prices followed by the first sizable imports of food in the country's history. According to Wilson, between 1922 and 1926 maize prices increased 100 percent, rice prices 300 percent, and bean prices 225 percent. Soon after, "maize and rice imports, which were negligible before 1928, began to be significant . . . and totaled 12,000 and 1,000 tons, respectively, in 1929. Previously, El Salvador imported less food than did any of the other Central American Republics" (1970: 126, 127).

By 1933 coffee occupied 96,523 hectares (33.7 percent) of the 286,545 hectares dedicated to El Salvador's principal crops (*Anuario* 1933). By 1966 that area had expanded to 140,100 hectares, ranking coffee a close second to maize (165,754 hectares) for cultivated area among all crops, a rank it has maintained ever since (*Indicadores* 1973). The nearly perfect competitive exclusion of maize from coffee-producing regions is shown in Figures 2.10 and 2.11. Note how the intensity of maize cultivation increases close to the excluded areas, a graphic illustration of something the pre-Columbian Indians well rec-ognized: the volcanic soils are the most fertile in the country.

To summarize to this point, aggregate statistics from El Salvador appear to provide evidence for the argument that rapid population growth accounts for the country's growing scarcity of food and land. As we have seen, however, the shortage of land nationally and for food-crop cultivators in particular is largely a problem of competitive allocation. Large expanses of fertile land have been converted to the production of export crops at the expense of domestic food produc-tion. It might be argued, to be sure, that from a balance-of-payments point of view the country as a whole is better off with land in export crops. But the problem is, as we shall see in the next section, that most Salvadoreans do not derive much benefit from export production.

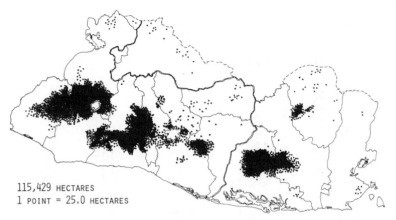

115,429 HECTARES
1 POINT = 25.0 HECTARES

Fig. 2.10. Coffee-growing areas of El Salvador, 1950. SOURCE: ESDGEC 1954: 59.

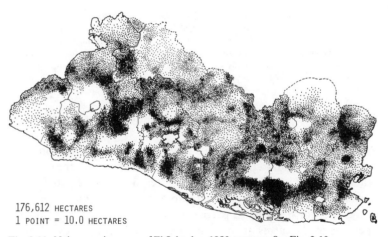

176,612 HECTARES
1 POINT = 10.0 HECTARES

Fig. 2.11. Maize-growing areas of El Salvador, 1950. SOURCE: See Fig. 2.10.

The Distribution of Farmland

As discussed in Chapter One, a Malthusian emphasis on a popula-
tion-resource imbalance assumes that distribution plays little or no
role in creating resource scarcity. Distributional dynamics are either
dismissed as "modifying factors" or ignored completely, the "power

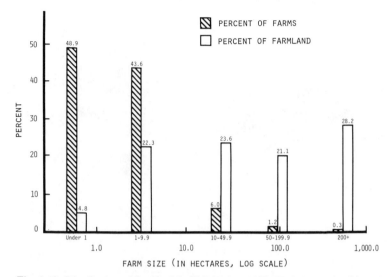

Fig. 2.12. Distribution of farmland in El Salvador, 1971. Each "percent of farms" histogram is centered at the point along the x-axis corresponding to the average size of all farms in that size class (for example, the average size of all farms in the under-1.0-hectare category is 0.53 hectares). A four-cycle logarithmic scale for the x-axis was necessary because of the extreme disparity among size classes of Salvadorean farms. SOURCE: ESDGEC 1975.

of population" being assumed to have an overpowering effect on all other causes of scarcity.

Figure 2.12 presents a serious challenge to this assumption in the case of El Salvador. The figure shows the distribution of the country's total farmland in 1971 (1,451,894 hectares) among its 270,868 farms, regardless of tenure, as grouped into five size categories. Three features are worth noting in particular, namely: (1) that more than 48 percent of the farms at that time were small units of less than 1.0 hectare; (2) that the 1.5 percent of all farms in the two largest categories (those with 50 hectares or more) held almost 50 percent of the total farmland; and (3) that the average farm in the largest size class was nearly 1,000 times the size of the average farm in the smallest class.

The dynamics of Salvadorean population growth have attracted a good deal of attention, but this distributional pattern, too, has a pronounced dynamic that has tended to be overlooked. In 1971, however, the geographer David Browning completed a careful study of historical trends in land use and land tenure in El Salvador. Using his analysis, we are able to distinguish three phases in the changeover from the pre-conquest "inheritance of social equality" to the extreme concentration shown in Figure 2.12.

Phase I: The pre-conquest and colonial periods. According to Browning:

To the Indian private and individual ownership of land was as meaningless as private ownership of the sky, the weather, or the sea. It is probable that the *capulli*, the oldest form of Aztec territorial organization and the basic unit of settlement, was used by the Pipil Indians of El Salvador. Each family of a clan group that shared the *capulli* had a right to use part of it under conditions laid down by the local chief, the *capullec*. No one had the right to cultivate a particular piece of land in perpetuity, and indeed the migratory nature of *milpa* farming discouraged this. The individual family was periodically allocated a plot within the area of land that the village regarded as for its own use. To this extent there was a sense of possession of land, but only as far as the use of land was concerned. (1971: 16)

Although there is some evidence of stratification and differential access to land among contemporary Indian families in Mesoamerica (see Cancian 1965), the communal pattern of land tenure in pre-conquest El Salvador was probably a relatively equitable system, exhibiting few if any major distributional inequalities. Indeed, as late as 1962 the anthropologist Alejandro Marroquín found that 58 percent of the Indian villagers of San Pedro Nonualco had access to 68 percent of the land within the municipal boundaries.

That village, however, has supposedly been less affected than most by post-conquest tenure changes. As Browning notes (1971: 33), "The Spaniard discovered, through conquest, possibilities for personal gain offered by a fertile land and its existing inhabitants, and viewed these two in terms of their exploitation." Beginning with the first Crown grants of *encomienda* between 1520 and 1530, Spanish settlers began a long-term process of encroachment on Indian communities and their communal lands. At first the encroachment took the form of a simple extraction of labor. The Spaniards did not themselves become involved in the production of balsam and cacao, two early export crops, but instead obtained their supply through Indian labor and tribute payments.

The pattern soon changed, however, with the introduction and commercial production of indigo (*Indigofera tinctoria* and *Indigofera suffruticosa*) in the second half of the sixteenth century. Land grants were obtained by Spanish colonists for the establishment of *haciendas de añil* (indigo), thereby beginning the process of "competition for land between the subsistence cultivator and the *hacendado* [that persisted] throughout the colonial period" (Browning 1971: 49). Even though these initial grants were generous, the hacendados often illegally extended their holdings to make room for more indigo cultivation and reserves and also to expand their grazing lands. Uncontrolled cattle ranging and a general state of confusion over rights, titles, and landmarks were apparently the principal means by which haciendas were expanded at the Indians' expense. As Browning puts it (p. 72): "One result of the Spanish organization of indigo production in the colony was the introduction of a number of individually owned estates that were gradually increased in size, invariably at the expense of lands cultivated by the Indian. As most of the areas suitable for indigo were already settled by Indian village communities, territorial competition between the private estate and the village was inevitable."

By 1770 there were more than 440 colonial haciendas incorporating or adjoining the Indians' pueblos. The land area they encompassed was substantial. In 1807, near the end of the colonial period, Gutiérrez y Ulloa estimated that the five largest estates ranged from roughly 1,400 hectares to nearly 6,000 hectares and totaled almost 19,000. Using 2,000 acres (809 hectares) as a modest average for these haciendas, and using 440 as a conservative total for the number of estates, Browning (1971: 84) estimates that the Spanish had appropriated almost one-third of the colony's land area. Although the Crown passed several ordinances to help preserve traditional communal lands and where necessary to create new collective tracts (called *ejidos*), many Indian villagers must have shared the experience of the inhabitants of Opico, who declared in a 1686 petition to colonial authorities: "We find ourselves short of land because of the many *haciendas* that have been or are being established very close to our village" (cited in *ibid.*, p. 106). By 1739 the Indian village of Opico had disappeared.

Phase II: The expansion of coffee. Despite these encroachments and land tenure changes, a good number of Indian villages managed to keep their communal and/or ejidal lands through the colonial period and into the first years of the Republic founded in 1839. Figure 2.13

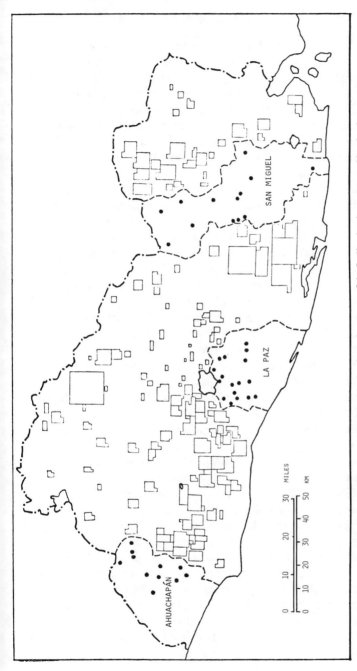

Fig. 2.13. Indian common lands in El Salvador, 1879. The blocks show the extent of the Indian lands as reported by the departments. The labeled departments did not provide any size estimates but simply identified the villages known to hold communal lands (shown by the dots). SOURCE: D. Browning 1971:191.

shows the extent of their common lands in 1879, as reported in a government survey. On the basis of the survey data, Browning concludes (1971: 192) that the villages regarded well over a quarter of the country as their domain. Much of this land was concentrated in the fertile volcanic highlands, traditionally the area of densest Indian settlement, a fact that was not lost on the government of the republic, or on the growing numbers of commercial coffee growers it represented. To them, communal lands represented an obstruction to the expansion of coffee plantations.

In 1881, just two years after this survey, the government abolished the traditional communal land system. The preamble to the official decree reads: "The existence of lands under the ownership of *comunidades* impedes agricultural development, obstructs the circulation of wealth, and weakens family bonds and the independence of the individual. Their existence is contrary to the economic and social principles that the Republic has accepted" (Law for the Extinction of Communal Lands, Feb. 26, 1881, cited in Browning 1971: 205; see also Torres 1961). Although the government's intention may have been to divide the land among those who had worked it, the result was more often than not the complete loss of traditional lands to private landowners, who proceeded to devote them exclusively to coffee. In more than one village, "The 1881 abolition of *tierras communales* merely legalized a process of alienation of [Indian] lands that was already well advanced" (Browning 1971: 207; see also Torres 1961, 1962; Marroquín 1965). In 1882 the ejidal system that had been established by colonial authorities was likewise abolished as "an obstacle to our agricultural development [and] contrary to our economic principles" (Law for the Extinction of Public Lands, March 2, 1882, cited in Torres 1961: 11–17). Claimants to ejidal parcels were initially given just six months to establish and pay for their legal title.

As a result of these self-styled Liberal Reform measures and the ensuing confusion over bureaucratic procedures for the issuance of lawful titles, large numbers of peasants were dispossessed of their lands. As mentioned earlier, the process was closely connected to the expansion of coffee. "With the extension of coffee cultivation . . . the traditional small land parcels were consolidated into large units, often lying fallow or producing export rather than subsistence crops" (E. A. Wilson 1970: 116). Many an evicted peasant was converted to "a dispossessed landless wanderer seeking work as a hired laborer on a [coffee] *finca* or hacienda" (Browning 1971: 219). Less than 20 years after these laws were enacted, the government itself recognized the problems it had created, attesting to the severity of the social dislocation. In 1896 the legislature passed a decree reconfirming full owner-ship rights for those agriculturalists who still held their communal land plots, since "public necessity requires their distribution among poor farmers" (cited in *ibid.*, p. 212).

Although this decree may have slowed the trend toward land concentration somewhat, it did not stop the expansion of coffee cultivation. A new wave of concentration was set off by a sudden drop in coffee prices in the late 1920's, when many of the smaller proprietors lost their land through defaults on loans and contractual debts. A few years later, as the depression deepened, an estimated 28 percent of the coffee holdings, primarily those of the small growers, changed hands (Marroquín, unpublished study; cited in Anderson 1971:9).

In 1928 a Salvadorean scholar, Alberto Masferrer, lamented the trend toward land concentration in his country:

About forty-five years ago, the land in the country was distributed among the majority of Salvadoreans, but now it is falling into the hands of a few owners. In other words, El Salvador is moving toward *latifundia* at a time when most countries are attempting to move away from it. With our population growing at the rate of 30,000 per year, to move toward *latifundia* is so unnecessary, dangerous, inhuman, and absurd that it can only be explained by the unhappy fact that long ago we stopped considering the need to think ahead (*Patria*, Dec. 29, 1928; cited in E. A. Wilson 1970: 121).

As might be expected, these rapid changes in El Salvador's land distribution provoked a series of popular uprisings centered in the areas of rapid coffee expansion. Noting the dates of five of these uprisings (1872, 1875, 1880, 1885, and 1898), Abelardo Torres (1962: 9) argues for a relationship of cause and effect between the loss of land and the rural workers' revolts. The largest uprising, described as one of the bloodiest in the history of Latin America by Thomas Anderson (1971), took place in 1932, shortly after the onset of the Great Depression and the second wave of land concentration related to coffee. That revolt, described in detail by Anderson, centered in and around the former Indian communities of Santa Ana, Ahuachapán, and Sonsonate — precisely those areas most affected by the Phase II dynamics.

During the revolt and its even more violent repression, called *la matanza* (the slaughter), about 1 percent of the Salvadorean population was killed. Another student of the period, Robert Elam, observed in 1968 that "awesome details of [the 1932] terrorism still remain clear in the minds of many Salvadoreans, and fear of a similar occurrence has in part shaped the legislation and policies of governments ever since 1932" (p. 44).

Phase III: The diversification of commercial agriculture. The value of coffee exports from El Salvador dropped precipitously during the Great Depression and 1932 revolt, from the equivalent of U.S. $22.7 million in 1928 to U.S. $6.4 million in 1932 (*Anuario* 1964: 3). Thereafter, the value remained below the 1928 figure well into the Second World War due to faltering prices on the world market.

Beginning in this period of stagnation, and continuing right up to the present, El Salvador has sought to diversify its agricultural exports and thereby reduce its economic dependence on coffee. As noted by Browning and studied in more detail by Ridgway Satterthwaite (1971), this diversification stimulated yet another phase of land concentration. The expansion of cotton production described above was partly responsible. Large areas of the Pacific lowlands were converted to cotton plantations in the 1950's and early 1960's as large landholders sought to take advantage of favorable market conditions. The economic value of land in this region increased rapidly, and this "greatly reduced the land area available to *campesinos* [peasants] whether they were *colonos* [hacienda laborers], sharecroppers, or renters," or indeed squatters (Satterthwaite 1971: 142). Even the cotton crash helped to consolidate landholdings for, as Satterthwaite notes, larger farms had higher survival rates during the crisis years.

Sugar production for export was another part of the diversification phase. The total land area planted annually in sugarcane increased from 10,000 hectares in the 1930's to 28,000 hectares by 1971 (*Anuario* 1933–39, 1971), and export production increased nearly 1,000 percent in the same period. As the agricultural censuses reveal, much of this expanded production took place on large holdings (over 50 hectares), where, once again, we may infer that tenant farmers were displaced. The expanded production of lesser commercial crops (tobacco and sesame in particular) has probably also contributed to the increasing concentration of land. By 1971 the distribution was extremely skewed, as shown in Figure 2.12.

A summary of distributional dynamics. The changes in the distribution of land brought about by the colonial period with its haciendas (Phase I), the coffee expansion period with its Liberal Reform measures (Phase II), and the post-Depression diversification of commercial agriculture (Phase III) are summarized in Figure 2.14. Access to farmland in Indian communities prior to the conquest probably approximated the even distribution shown by the dashed diagonal line. For the curve summarizing Phase II, I made three assumptions: (1) that any land affected by distributional dynamics was planted in coffee by 1932; (2) that coffee land tenure was proportionately the same in 1932 as in 1938, when the first national coffee census was taken; and (3) that the effects of Phase II were additive to those of Phase I. The histogram used to indicate the changes in land distribution for Phase III is derived from agricultural census figures for 1971.

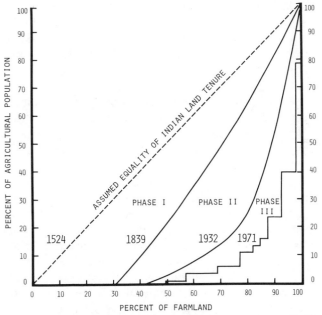

Fig. 2.14. The dynamics of land concentration in El Salvador, 1524–1971. The histogram for Phase III allows for 138,031 landless workers in 1971 (21.8 percent of the agricultural population). SOURCE: Phase I, D. Browning 1971. Phase II, Asociación Cafetalera de El Salvador 1940. Phase III, ESDGEC 1975, 1977.

For this curve, I have assumed a figure of 1.8 full-time agricultural workers for each farm unit reported in the census. The curve also allows for 138,031 landless agriculturalists, calculated as the difference between the economically active population in agriculture— 632,054 as given by ESDGEC 1977—and the number of permanent agricultural workers reported in ESDGEC 1975—494,023. It is apparent from the figure that land concentration has been a dynamic influence on resource scarcity in El Salvador (compare with Fig. 1.3B).

Comparing the Causes of Land Scarcity

With the data assembled in preceding sections, we can now compare the relative influence of population growth and land concentration on the scarcity of land in El Salvador. As an estimate of the total land available in the country for agricultural purposes I use 1,580,000 hectares (the "total land in farms," according to the 1961 census; this total was lower in 1971). From this, I subtract 355,000 hectares, as an estimate of the land in large holdings (haciendas) before 1892, based on Browning's study. This leaves 1,225,000 hectares as the land base subject to post-1892 competitive dynamics. Dividing this figure by 165,400, the 1892 economically active population in agriculture (from Table 2.2) yields 7.41 hectares as the average land area available to each agriculturalist in 1891. Likewise, assuming an agricultural population of 632,054 in 1971, I obtain 1.94 hectares per agriculturalist in 1971.* I then divide the two figures to arrive at 3.82 as the shrinkage due to population growth in the interval, a number that can be called the "population factor."

Table 2.3 compares the land base predicted for 1971 on the basis of population growth with the actual land bases reported in the 1971 census for the agriculturally active population (the landless agricultural population is estimated as for Fig. 2.14). The table shows the average amount of land available per agriculturalist in 1971 by farm-size categories. The 3.82 population factor, as well as a "distribution factor," is shown for each category. Representing the additional shrinkage of land due to distributional dynamics, the distribution factor is calculated as the ratio of the 1971 national average land base

---

* It should be emphasized that these figures represent the average amount of land potentially available per agriculturalist for these years, excluding hacienda holdings.

TABLE 2.3 *The Dynamics of Land Scarcity in El Salvador, 1892–1971*

Farm size in hectares	1971 census figures for the agriculturally active population			Land shrinkage between 1892 and 1971 due to:		
	Distribution of population		Average hectares of land per person	Population factor	Distribution factor	Combined factor
	Percent	Cumulative percent				
Landless	21.8%	21.8%	—	3.82	∞	∞
<1.0	29.0	50.8	0.38	3.82	5.11	19.50
1.0–1.99	15.6	66.4	0.82	3.82	2.37	9.04
2.0–2.99	8.0	74.4	1.21	3.82	1.60	6.12
3.0–3.99	3.3	77.7	1.66	3.82	1.17	4.46
4.0–4.99	2.8	80.5	2.08	3.82	+1.07	3.56
5.0–9.99	5.7	86.1	3.10	3.82	+1.60	2.39

SOURCE: Total available land for agriculture based on ESDGEC 1967; 1892 agriculturally active population estimated from Barberena 1892 and Table 2.2; 1971 agriculturally active population from ESDGEC 1975; landless population in 1971 calculated as the difference between the economically active population in agriculture and the total number of permanent agricultural workers from ESDGEC 1975 and 1977; agriculturally active population by farm-size category from ESDGEC 1975.

NOTE: The population factor is obtained by dividing the 1892 national average land area per agriculturalist (7.41 hectares) by the 1971 figure (1.94 hectares). The distribution factor is calculated by dividing the 1971 average figure by the average number of hectares per agriculturalist in a given farm-size category. The combined factor can be read as follows: for the 50.8 percent of the agriculturally active population with access to less than 1.0 hectare of land, there has been at least a 19.50-fold decrease in land availability between 1892 and 1971.

(1.94 hectares) to the average land area per farm-size category. For example, farms of less than 1.0 hectare averaged 0.38 hectare per agriculturalist—a figure that is about one-fifth (1:5.11) of the 1971 national average. The *total* reduction in the land base from 1892 to 1971 for each farm-size category, called the "combined factor," is calculated as the 1892 national average (7.41 hectares) divided by the category average.

The data in Table 2.3 show that the effects of land concentration (the distribution factor) have been greater than the effects of rapid population growth (the population factor) for a full 50.8 percent of the agricultural population of El Salvador. For these people, the hypothetical 1892 land base of 7.41 hectares shrank to an average of 0.38 hectare or less by 1971—a 19.5-fold decrease in land availability. Distributional dynamics figured larger than population dynamics in that change by a ratio of 1.34:1 (5.11 against 3.82), or more. More-

over, the table shows that a full 77.7 percent of the agricultural population (i.e., through the 3–3.99-hectare size class) experienced a
scarcity greater than that generated by population growth alone.
Conversely, about 22.3 percent of the agricultural population were
protected from the full impact of population growth by favorable
distributional changes after 1892.

Figure 2.15 shows this comparison of the dynamics behind scarcity
in two distinct conceptualizations. Both diagrams represent, to scale,
the land area calculations of Table 2.3 for the 50.8 percent of El Salvador's economically active population in 1971 that was landless or
land-poor (defined as those with farm plots of less than 1.0 hectare).
Figure 2.15A first applies the population factor to the 1892 land base,
reducing the average land available per economically active agriculturalist to 1.94 hectares in 1971, and then allows for the "modifying"
influence of land concentration. Conceptualized in this fashion, population growth appears to account for the greater part of the land
shrinkage from 1892 to 1971. It appears that a hypothetical 5.47 hectares of the original 7.41 were lost to population growth, and only 1.56
to land concentration. This is essentially a neo-Malthusian interpretation of the data.

Because the distribution factor is actually the larger of the two factors, the dynamics of land scarcity for this subpopulation are more
accurately portrayed by Figure 2.15B. In this case, the effects of land
concentration are shown first (shrinking the 7.41 hectares of 1892 to a
hypothetical 1.45 hectares), and population is then added as the modifying influence. In this conceptualization, 5.96 hectares are absorbed
by land concentration, and only 1.07 are lost to population growth.
Distributional dynamics, therefore, provides a better single-factor
explanation than population dynamics for the land scarcity experienced by the bulk of El Salvador's agricultural population. At the
same time, however, the figure also makes it clear that neither population growth nor land concentration alone provides an adequate explanation of that scarcity. The data most closely conform to the combination model of resource scarcity described in Chapter One.

To summarize, in this hemisphere's most densely populated mainland country, it was not so much the rapid growth of the population
after 1892 as the simultaneous trend toward land concentration that
created a scarcity of land for the majority of the agricultural popula-

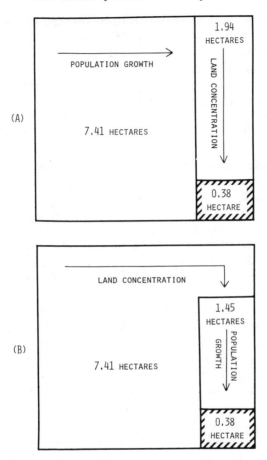

Fig. 2.15. The dynamics of land scarcity for the landless and land-poor of El Salvador, 1892–1971. Diagram B, based on Table 2.3, applies the larger of the two factors, land concentration, first, as opposed to Diagram A, a neo-Malthusian interpretation of the data.

tion prior to the conflict with Honduras. This, of course, does not deny that population growth contributed to the shortage of land, nor does it mean that population growth will indefinitely remain second in importance. Indeed, recent analysts (e.g., CELADE 1974; Fox & Huguet 1977) predict a sustained average population growth rate in the country of 3.2 percent per year between 1971 and 2000, and a total population of 8,800,000 at the end of the period. If their predictions prove valid, the population factor could conceivably surpass the distribution factor in the next few decades. Nevertheless, in the decades leading up to the Soccer War, the data indicate that land scarcity was more the product of land concentration. Ironically, to recognize population pressure as a serious problem behind the conflict is to acknowledge that land concentration has been a problem of even greater magnitude.

The combined effects of these two factors through time have caused an extremely rapid competitive exclusion of rural inhabitants from the land base. In Table 2.4 we observe that in the 11 years between 1950 and 1961 the proportion of "excluded" people (i.e., the landless and the land-poor) rose by almost nine percentage points. Moreover, in these pre–Soccer War years their annual rate of growth—3.45 per-cent—was 1.2 times the national rate (2.81 percent) and 1.6 times the rate for the agriculturally active population as a whole. Between 1961 and 1971 the excluded population increased another 3.5 percentage points while growing at 3.35 percent annually. Total population growth was slightly higher in this period (3.49 percent annually), but one reason for this was a high rate of rural out-migration among the landless and land-poor, as discussed below. Even so, the excluded population increased 1.8 times faster than the agriculturally active population and 1.2 times faster than the rural population as a whole.

T A B L E 2.4 *Competitive Exclusion of the Rural Population in El Salvador, 1950–1971*

Agriculturally active population	1950	1961	1971
Landless	53,015	75,632	138,031
Land-poor (<1.0 hectare)	105,654	154,267	183,002
TOTAL (percent of agriculturally active population)	158,669 (38.5%)	229,899 (47.3%)	321,033 (50.8%)

SOURCE: Landless, 1950 and 1971, calculated as the difference between the economically active population in agriculture and the total number of permanent agricultural workers, from ESDGEC 1953, 1954, 1975, 1977. Landless, 1961, from CEPAL 1971: 67–68. Land-poor, 1950, 1961, and 1971, from ESDGEC 1954, 1967, 1975.

These figures make it clear that resource competition is not simply a density-dependent process in El Salvador. For years before the conflict with Honduras, the agricultural population experienced a scarcity of resources that cannot be explained by population growth.

Additional Consequences of Land Scarcity

Land-Use Patterns

In 1965 Esther Boserup hypothesized that where land scarcity arises from population pressure one would expect to find intensive land-use practices, particularly on good and fertile soils. Since then, this expectation has been substantiated by several studies, including most notably Harner 1970, Vermeer 1970, Spooner 1972, and Barlett 1975. Accordingly, in a country as densely inhabited and rapidly growing as El Salvador, we could reasonably expect to find all but the very poorest soils and steepest slopes fully cultivated.

But again because of land distribution, this is not what one finds. Figure 2.16 shows the percentage of all land under cultivation in 1961 by farm-size category. The farm-size categories correspond to those of Figure 2.12, and again the abscissa is logarithmic with four cycles. It is clear from the figure that truly intensive land use was confined to the small farms, particularly those under 1.0 hectare. Farms of more than 50 hectares accounted for nearly 60 percent of El Salvador's total farmland and cultivated less than 35 percent of this area. In fact, 45.8 percent of all the land in these farms was used for pasture (416,365 of 909,204 hectares). Moreover, a full 32 percent of the land classified as under cultivation on these farms was actually fallow in that year. (ESDGEC 1967: 206).

Figure 2.16 also presents evidence that extensive land use is not required by soil qualities or other ecological conditions specific to large estates. The shaded histograms represent maize yields as a function of farm size as reported in the 1961 census (maize is often used as a standard for plant growth comparisons in ecological studies). The average yield per hectare of maize planted on farms of over 100 hectares is 1.65 times greater than the average yield of maize on plots under 1.0 hectare.

Contrary to expectations, Figure 2.16 therefore indicates that areas of good and fertile soil are used relatively extensively. Because of the

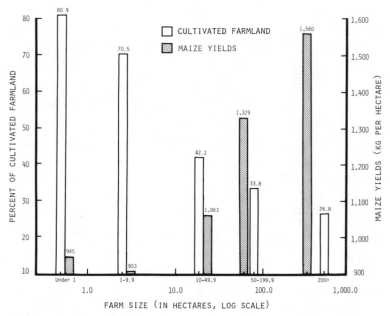

Fig. 2.16. Intensive land use and average maize yields by farm size in El Salvador, 1961. The maize-yield histograms lie to the left of the land-use histograms for the two largest farm sizes because of differences in the categories used in reporting them: 50.0–99.9 and 100 and over hectares, and 50.0–199.9 and 200 and over, respectively. SOURCE: ESDGEC 1967.

land distribution, it is often on the very poorest soils and steepest slopes that one finds highly intensive land use in El Salvador. This confirms Ernest Feder's general observation (1971: 30) that in Latin America "land is a scarce resource only for the small holders."

Actually, the situation is even more exaggerated than the histograms of Figure 2.16 imply. Turning again to the data in the 1961 agricultural census, we find that even when large landholders do use land for cultivation, it is generally to produce export crops. Figure 2.17 shows the relationship between crop production and farm size for the most important food crop, maize, and the most important export crop, coffee. As we see, small farms contribute disproportionately to the production of food crops, and large farms contribute the

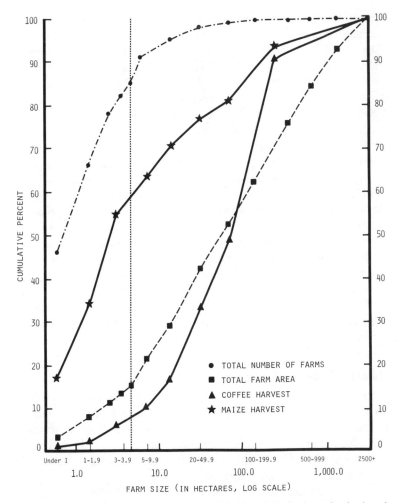

Fig. 2.17. Crop production by farm size in El Salvador, 1961. As shown by the dotted vertical line, farms of less than 5.0 hectares produced 58 percent of all the maize on 15.6 percent of the farmland. SOURCE: ESDGEC 1967.

greater share of export products. Consider, for example, the land area and production figures for farms of less than five hectares (as shown by the dotted line). These farms constitute 85.2 percent of all farms but include only 15.6 percent of the farmland. On that 15.6 percent, they produce about 58 percent of all the maize in the country but only about 8 percent of the coffee. In contrast, the 2,148 farms with over 100 hectares (0.9 percent of the total number) occupy 47.7 percent of the total area, but produce only 19.1 percent of the maize, compared with 51.2 percent of the coffee.

To summarize to this point, the evidence reviewed in this chapter leads to the conclusion that the scarcity of food and the scarcity of land in El Salvador are not the simple products of population growth. First, we find that food is scarce not because the land is incapable of producing enough for the resident population, but rather because large areas have been underutilized or dedicated to the production of export crops. Second, we find that land is scarce not because there is too little to go around, but rather because of a process of competitive exclusion by which the small farmers have been increasingly squeezed off the land—a process due as much to the dynamics of land concentration as to population pressure. Land-use patterns show that land is not scarce for large landholders.

Rural Out-Migration

In a previous section we saw that the number of landless and land-poor in El Salvador has been growing faster than the country's total population. This finding of itself stands as a serious challenge to simple population pressure explanations of resource scarcity. However, it becomes still more problematical for that interpretation when rural out-migration is taken into account.

Table 2.5 presents a very conservative set of estimates for the rural out-migration implied by El Salvador's census data. For these estimates I have used the methodology of R. P. Shaw (1976), calculating the annual out-migration rates as the difference between total and rural population growth. Although useful as a first approximation, particularly in the absence of more reliable information, this procedure provides at best a minimum estimate. For example, in the 1971 Salvadorean census rural women in the 45–49 age group had an average of 5.32 living children, compared with only 3.94 for urban women

TABLE 2.5 *Estimated Rural Out-Migration in El Salvador, 1892–1971*

	Rural population [a]		Rural out-migration		Urban population		
Year	Total	Average annual growth rate in the interval	Average annual rate per 1,000 [b]	Number of migrants in the interval [c]	Total	Average annual growth rate in the interval	Percent of urban growth due to rural migration
1892	562,800	1.86%	0.43	18,400	140,700	2.06%	11.20%
1930	1,129,328	1.00	2.96	83,300	305,033	2.26	48.17
1950	1,377,951	2.30	5.06	97,800	477,966	4.14	36.71
1961	1,766,601	2.91	5.81	138,600	744,383	4.76	30.93
1971	2,362,173				1,192,475		

SOURCE: Barberena 1892; ESDGEC 1942, 1953, 1967, 1974a.

[a] Recalculated from census information as described in Table 2.2.

[b] Difference between the growth rates of the total population and the rural population.

[c] Difference between the actual rural population and the projected rural population as based on growth rate of the total population.

of the same ages (ESDGEC 1974a: 437). Calculating rural out-migration on the basis of an average national growth rate effectively ignores this difference and assumes an average of 4.68 living children for all women of those ages. Nevertheless, this conservative estimation procedure has important implications for interpreting the scarcity of land in El Salvador.

As shown in the table, a rural exodus was evident as early as the 1892–1930 intercensal period. In that interval an estimated 18,400 rural inhabitants migrated to urban centers, accounting for 11.20 percent of the total urban growth over the period. The inferred annual out-migration rate increased almost seven times in the next 20 years, and climbed still further in the next decade. By the 1961–71 period the rate was higher than 5.8 persons per 1,000, implying an intercensal total of 138,600 departures by 1971. This means that between 1892 and the census date of 1971, a minimum total of 338,100 rural dwellers moved to El Salvador's urban centers. Yet though the cities grew at an average annual rate of more than 4 percent between 1950 and 1971, we can see in the table that the calculated rural-urban migration accounts for only some 30–35 percent of the total urban growth. This is further evidence of the conservative nature of the migration estimates produced by Shaw's method, for in other Central American Countries this figure is often estimated at over 50 percent (see, e.g., Brunn & Thomas 1973, on Honduras).

At the very least, then, 97,800 rural persons migrated to urban areas in the period 1950–61. Of this total, it is reasonable to infer (from Table 2.2) that at least 28 percent, or some 27,400 persons, had been economically active in agriculture. If, as Shaw argues for other Latin American countries (and see Chapter Three below), the vast majority of these were landless and land-poor peasants, the figure of 229,899 for the excluded population in 1961 (Table 2.4) is at least 12 percent too low. In fact, I think it is probably lower by much more, since Shaw, using a different formula based on rural vital statistics for the 1950–61 period (unfortunately not available for earlier periods), has calculated a net rural-urban migration of 176,854 persons for El Salvador for those years (1976: 5). By this estimate, my excluded population figure for 1961 would be 22 percent too low, since it ignores urban out-migration.

These calculations of internal migration in El Salvador have three important implications for the study of the ecological origins of the Soccer War. First, they imply that my representation of the process of competitive exclusion in El Salvador is extremely conservative. By ignoring landless and land-poor rural-urban migrants in weighing the respective roles of land concentration and population growth in generating scarcity, I have effectively biased the data in favor of the neo-Malthusian interpretation. But even with this bias, Table 2.3 indicates that population pressure is an inadequate and misleading explanation of El Salvador's land scarcity.

Second, these calculations show that rural-urban migration both began very early (i.e., years before the aggregate-level land crises shown in Fig. 2.5) and grew at an increasing rate. If this migration can indeed be linked to land shortage, as I believe, then we would have still more evidence for an accelerating process of competitive exclusion in rural areas. The relationship of land scarcity to migration will be examined in more detail in Chapter Three.

Finally, Table 2.5 deals only with the internal rural-urban migration that is implied by national census information. The data do not make any allowance for rural out-migration to Honduras, which is, after all, one of the central concerns of this study. They do, however, permit an important inference: *if* rural-urban migration within El Salvador is largely a response to the resource scarcity confronting poor peasants, and *if* rural out-migration to Honduras is largely a response to the same conditions, then these internal migration estimates should be roughly proportional to the numbers of Salvadoreans resident in Honduras before 1969.

Various estimates of that immigrant population provide support for this hypothesis. According to Everett Wilson, the consolidation of coffee holdings in El Salvador in the 1920's stimulated a sharp increase in the migration of poor rural dwellers to urban areas, and also to Honduras. He estimates that by the late 1920's the number of Salvadoreans in Honduras exceeded 12,000, and that they "comprised perhaps as much as 10 percent of the total labor force" there (1970: 129). The rate of migration and therefore of population and labor loss was alarming to some writers even before the decade had ended. In 1925 J. Alberto Herrera counseled: "In order to stop the emigration of Salvadoreans, every available measure must be taken to assure the well-being and improvement . . . of the workers, so that they will find

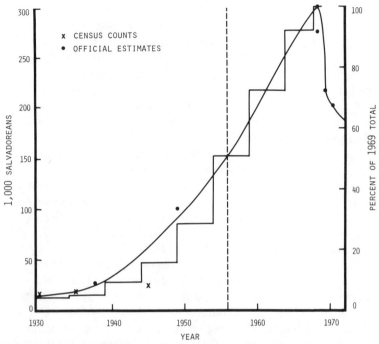

Fig. 2.18. Estimates of the Salvadorean population in Honduras, 1930–1972. The histogram represents a cumulative frequency plot for year of migration among a sample of Salvadorean refugees expelled from Honduras in 1969. The smooth curve indicates the general trend of the Salvadorean emigration to Honduras suggested by census counts, official estimates, and the refugee data. The dotted line shows that at least half of the immigrants who were in Honduras in 1969 had moved there by the mid-1950's. SOURCE: Migrants, late 1930's, Waterston 1949: 3, Barón Castro 1978: 584; early 1969 (250,000), Monteforte Toledo 1972: 91, de Paredes et al. 1969: 1; late 1969 (300,000), Guerrero 1969: 32. Returnees, CONAPLAN 1969: 5. Refugees, de Paredes et al. 1969: 15.

their work enjoyable. Entire families migrate, abandoning their work and depriving the country of their skills that could be used in developing the nation" ("La Emigración Salvadoreña, *Patria;* cited in E. A. Wilson 1970: 128). Four years later, Alberto Masferrer found "the problem of the *campesinos* and workers who emigrate to Honduras . . . chaotic" ("El Porque de la Emigración," *Patria*, cited in *ibid.*, p. 129). It is important to note that this migration, which began even as early as the turn of the century, was already accelerating in the 1920's and 1930's—near the end of coffee's rapid growth phase and more than 20 years before the onset of the Malthusian crisis indicated by the aggregate data.

Figure 2.18 presents a compilation of the estimates of the Salvadorean immigrant population in Honduras from 1930 to 1972. X's indicate actual census counts of persons living in Honduras who admitted to a Salvadorean birthplace (1930, 18,522; 1935, 19,268; and 1945, 23,029; not shown is the 1926 census figure of 13,452). The dots represent the following "informed estimates": (1) in the late 1930's the Consul General of El Salvador in Honduras estimated that there were 25,000 to 30,000 Salvadoreans in Honduras; (2) a confidential report on the economy of El Salvador in 1949 by the International Bank for Reconstruction and Development noted that Honduras had absorbed an estimated 100,000 Salvadoreans; (3) early in 1969 the Ministry of Foreign Relations in El Salvador estimated that there were 250,000 Salvadoreans residing in Honduras; and (4) later that year the ministry, in its statement of the *Position of El Salvador Before the Inter-American Commission on Human Rights*, revised the total number upward to 300,000.

Official estimates of returning refugees have also been included in the figure. El Salvador's National Planning Office estimated that 81,159 refugees had returned by December 1969; another 16,585 were expected by March 1970, and a cumulative long-range total of 130,000 was anticipated by that agency. The Honduran census figures for 1950 (20,285) and 1961 (38,002) have not been included for two reasons. First, contrary to common practice and official estimates, children born in Honduras to Salvadorean parents were counted as Hondurans. This technicality results in a cumulative underestimation: children born to the 1930–45 generation of immigrants were not counted in 1950 or 1961. Second, we might reasonably expect an increasing reluctance on the part of the immigrants and their children to admit their Salvadorean birth once political tensions began to build between the countries. Charles Teller (1972) encountered this problem while interviewing Salvadorean citizens in a random sample of barrio residents in San Pedro Sula, Honduras.

In addition to these estimates and census totals, Figure 2.18 includes a frequency histogram based on the work of Querubina de

Paredes and her associates (1969), the only existing quantitative study of war refugees. The histogram shows the cumulative proportion of migrants in their sample according to the date (in five-year intervals) of their departure for Honduras. These data were obtained in interviews with 140 heads of refugee families at a Red Cross station and refugee camp near San Salvador in the summer of 1969. By themselves, data from so small a sample could be considered only suggestive at best. However, they are clearly in close agreement with our informed estimates, and for the purposes of this analysis we may take them as a confirmation of those estimates. A reasonable approximation of the total immigrant population in Honduras is then given by the smooth curve in the figure.

On the basis of interval estimates from this curve, the influx of migrants to Honduras does appear very similar to the flow of rural-urban migration within the country (see Table 2.6). The interval percentages are very similar (the maximum discrepancy is only 7.17 percentage points), and even the raw totals are comparable. Judging from these estimates, it is almost as if for every two persons leaving El Salvador's rural areas in these years, one migrated to Honduras and the other migrated to urban areas within El Salvador. The minor differences between the internal and external migration figures, moreover, are consistent with expectations from the influence of other variables. Thus, in 1950–61, when there was a boom in Honduran commercial agriculture (see Chapter Four), large numbers of Salvadoreans went to Honduras as contract laborers for the expanding cotton estates (Capa & Stycos 1974), and the cities attracted fewer migrants. Likewise, in the following decade, when tensions mounted between the countries, the cityward migration surpassed the flow to Honduras.

From this evidence, one may tentatively conclude that there was indeed an association between the internal and external migration flows. This finding is consistent with the hypothesis that both are related to the land-scarcity problems of the small farmers in El Salvador. In the case of the migrants to Honduras, we have several additional pieces of evidence that many of these people did in fact come from the landless and land-poor group. To begin with, 86 of the 140 family heads (61.4 percent) interviewed in the de Paredes study stated that they had been landless wage laborers (*jornaleros*) before their

T A B L E 2.6 *Estimated Internal and External Migration of Salvadoreans,*
1892–1969

Period	Internal migration[a]		External migration[b]		Difference in percentage points
	Number of migrants in the interval	Percent of 1969 total	Number of migrants in the interval	Percent of 1969 total	
1892–1930	18,400	6.09%	18,500	6.17%	+.08
1930–50	83,300	27.59	81,500	27.16	−.43
1950–61	97,800	32.40	118,700	39.57	+7.17
1961–69	102,400 [c]	33.92	81,300	27.10	−6.82
TOTAL	301,900	100.00	300,000	100.00	

SOURCE: Internal migration, see Table 2.5. External migration, see Fig. 2.18.
[a] Does not include temporary or seasonal migration.
[b] Estimated migration of Salvadoreans to Honduras (Fig. 2.18).
[c] Interpolated from the 1961-71 data in Table 2.5.

departure, and 19 others (13.6 percent) described themselves as un-
skilled workers (*obreros no calificados*). Of this total of 105 persons, 86,
or 81.9 percent, became small farmers in Honduras (*agricultores en
pequeño*), implying that they had worked a plot of land for themselves.
As we shall see in Chapter Three, many of these same migrants had
actually come to own their land in Honduras before 1969. In addition,
the same study reported that 51.5 percent of the family heads said
their departure from El Salvador was originally motivated by unemployment. Another 43.5 percent claimed they were seeking to im-
prove their economic situation.

In another study, men who had been expelled from Honduras in
1969 were asked why they had left El Salvador in the first place. Some
of the typical responses were:

I had been renting about eight *manzanas* here [1 manzana = 1.7 acres
= 0.7 hectares]. I had cows and oxen, but they sold the hacienda, and I
could find no one to rent me land. It's terrible here.

I went to Honduras six years ago because you couldn't rent land here.

We were under the domination of the rich; we couldn't afford the rent they
were asking for land.

It used to be that the rich would rent you land and take part of the crop in
return. Now they only rent to the cotton growers, not to the poor.

I had to pay $24 per *manzana* rent for growing corn. In Honduras I rented
land for $1.50.

I rented about three *manzanas* at $20 each per year, and in addition I had to give the owner four sacks of grain per *manzana*, hardly leaving us enough to eat for the home. Then cotton came and you couldn't even rent at that price. (Capa & Stycos 1974: 44)

Finally, El Salvador's National Planning Office, in its study of the Salvadoreans expelled from Honduras, estimated that a full 76.9 percent of all the economically active members of the refugee population were agriculturalists (CONAPLAN 1969). Taken together, these estimates and reports indicate that many of the Salvadorean migrants to Honduras were small farmers, and that a large share of them had come from El Salvador's mounting total of landless and land-poor (see also Vieytez 1969; Fuentes Rivera 1971). In addition, the comments of the refugees cited above indicate that the expansion of cotton cultivation and increasing land rents were important influences on their decision to migrate.

To conclude, let me emphasize two features of Figure 2.18 that relate to the earlier discussion of land scarcity in El Salvador. First, the figure shows that the migration involved not only increasing numbers of Salvadoreans, but also increasing rates of migration. Exponential growth is detectable as early as 1940, and the growth rate does not appear to taper off until the tensions of the late 1960's. Second, the figure indicates that perhaps as many as half of the 1969 migrant total had already moved into Honduras by the mid-1950's (as shown by the dotted line). Neither of these trends is compatible with a Malthusian interpretation of El Salvador's land shortage. Indeed, the aggregate data of Figure 2.5 imply that the scarcity of land for food production and for subsistence farmers was both relatively minor and fairly constant until 1955. But by that time a good part of the emigration had already occurred, and it had long proceeded at accelerating rates. These developments are better explained by the alternative hypotheses proposed here. As a further test of these hypotheses and to understand better who the migrants were and why they migrated, I conducted the village study described in the next chapter.

CHAPTER THREE

Scarcity and Survival in Tenancingo

The national statistics presented in the previous chapter, though useful for an overview of the nature of land scarcity in El Salvador, do not provide sufficient detail for testing the hypothesized relationships between scarcity, survival, and migration outlined in Chapter One. In this chapter, we will investigate two basic ecological questions. First, does access to land directly influence the ability of peasants and their children to survive and reproduce? Second, is survival a major motivating factor for the two types of rural out-migration we have discussed, rural-urban migration and the migration of Salvadoreans to Honduras?

In an attempt to get the answers to these questions, I conducted an intensive local-level study in the small, rural community of Tenancingo, in El Salvador, where I (and my assistants) interviewed 285 peasant families. The study was designed to elicit information on two generations of family history for each household, so that I could analyze not only the ecological conditions that currently confront Salvadorean peasants (i.e., access to land in terms of quantity, quality, and stability), but also the ways in which the peasants have adapted to changes in these conditions. This chapter summarizes the results of that survey, focusing specifically on the relationship between family land base, demography, and migration.

Physical and Historical Features of Tenancingo

The municipality of Tenancingo, in the department of Cuscatlán, was chosen as a suitably representative study site on the basis of five criteria: (1) an average farm size well below the national average (reflecting the relative absence of large estates); (2) a land distribution in the small farm-size classes roughly equivalent to the national distribu-

T A B L E 3.1 *Selection Criteria for the El Salvador Study Site*

	1971 census figures	
Criteria	National average	Tenancingo
Average farm size (hectares)	5.36	2.82
Distribution of cropland under 50 hectares (percent)[a]		
<1.0 hectare	19.2%	21.6%
1.0–4.9 hectares	46.7	50.5
5.0–9.9 hectares	13.5	13.0
10.0–19.9 hectares	10.0	12.2
20.0–49.9 hectares	11.6	2.7
Owner-operated farms (percent)	39.9%	46.1%
Land use (percent)		
Perennial crops	11.3%	2.6%
Annual export crops	7.8	2.0
Annual non-export crops	26.8	45.2
Pasture	38.2	37.5
Woodland and scrub	11.6	8.3
Other	5.3	4.4
Average yields (kilograms/hectare)		
Maize (hybrid)	3,220	3,338
Maize (other)	1,467	1,183
Sorghum	1,244	1,069
Beans	1,336	829

SOURCE: ESDGEC 1974.

[a] The distribution of cropland is used as an estimate of the distribution of farm size, which is unavailable at the municipio level in El Salvador. As Fig. 2.16 indicates, this estimate is most accurate in the smaller farm-size categories.

tion (to ensure adequate variability for analysis); (3) a relatively high proportion of farms operated by their owners (to ensure a sample of families with relatively stable land bases); (4) a land-use pattern oriented heavily toward the cultivation of basic food crops rather than export crops; and (5) an average yield of basic food crops no greater than the national average. See Table 3.1 for the comparative figures.

Located near the geographic center of El Salvador, 30 kilometers northeast of the capital city (Fig. 2.9), the municipality covers roughly 53 square kilometers of hilly country, most of it between 400 and 600 meters above sea level, and receives 1,800 to 2,200 mm of rainfall annually, concentrated in a rainy season lasting from May through October (IGN 1973). Though the area was once covered by a tropical

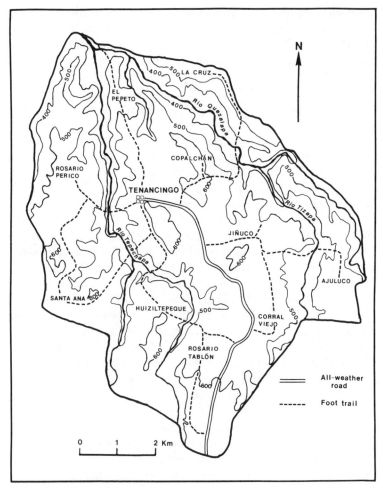

Fig. 3.1. The municipality of Tenancingo, El Salvador. Contour lines every 100 meters.

deciduous forest, by the mid-nineteenth century there was "little wood left for construction" (López 1858: 126).

According to one interpretation, the name Tenancingo derives from a Nahaut term meaning "area of many small valleys or walls" (IGN 1973). This is a title it well deserves. As shown in Figure 3.1, the municipality is dissected by the eroded valleys of two rivers (the

Quezalapa and the Tepechapa) and by numerous small creeks and ravines. In contrast to the relatively rich volcanic soil of the highland areas to the south and west, the soil is poor and acidic. Early visitors to Tenancingo commented that "the rugged terrain produces little and is good for little" (Cortez y Larraz 1770: 247), and that "the land is just as rocky as it is uneven" (López 1858: 125). This explains why slightly less of the total land area is held in farms than the national average (62.3 percent in 1971, compared with 69.0 percent nationally).

Tenancingo has just over 10,000 habitants; only 16 percent (1,600) of them reside in the central village, with the rest living in the ten surrounding *cantones* (hamlets) shown in Figure 3.1. The community has had regular bus service to San Salvador since 1945 via an all-weather road that connects with the Pan-American Highway 12 kilometers to the south. Before that, pack mules were the principal means of transport out of the village. Even today, only the three hamlets that border the road are accessible by motor vehicle. Foot trails and ox-cart paths connect the other hamlets to the village center and to each other.

The village itself is a picturesque example of Spanish colonial architecture and design, modified only in the early 1970's by the establishment of various national government offices. White-washed adobe buildings with clay-tile roofs are clustered in a rectangular grid around the church and the village square. The cobblestone streets are partially lined with the surviving orange trees planted by the Spanish settlers.

The village is the hub of the region's social, administrative, and economic activities. The most important public buildings are the Catholic church, which dates to the eighteenth century, judging from baptismal records; the municipal government office and jail, rebuilt in modern cement style; the two schoolhouses, one a primary school and the other a three-year secondary school; the health center, maintained by a resident nurse since its opening in 1967; the telephone and telegraph office; the agricultural extension office; and the headquarters of the Guardia Nacional (the national police force). There are seven *tiendas* (general stores), as well as a central marketplace, two pharmacies, three licensed outlets for aguardiente, one cantina, and a meeting-place for the local chapter of Alcoholics Anonymous. In addition to these establishments and three small hat factories (described below), a limited amount of nonfarm employment is provided by several bakeries and shops belonging to tailors, carpenters, and other artisans. The village has had running water since 1945 (although without a sewer) and electricity since 1964.

The village of Tenancingo in the Department of Cuscatlán, El Salvador. The river Tepechapa lies just beyond the last row of buildings.

A peasant family house, or choza. *Sleeping quarters are directly behind the kitchen with its clay tile roof. Animals, including dogs, chickens, and pigs, are kept in the yard, or* solar, *which is surrounded by plots of maize. The barrels are used to collect rainwater and to store grains.*

Above, left. *This peasant woman and her two young sons are making* trenzas (*braids*) *of palm, which will be sold for a few cents each to be factory-stitched into hats. Trenzas are made in virtually all rural Tenancingo households and are a major source of cash income. The little girl holds her breakfast, a salted tortilla made of sorghum.* Above, right. *A tenant farmer displays three of his most important agricultural tools: a hoe, a digging stick, and a wooden plow.*

Below. *Three of the four children in this landless family have the distended bellies indicative of malnutrition.*

The landscape around Tenancingo is a checkerboard mosaic of small family farms, typical of peasant communities in rural El Salvador.

A hillside of rented plots just south of the village. Most of the land shown here belongs to one proprietor, who rents out small parcels on a yearly basis to local peasant families.

Land scarcity in rural El Salvador has caused widespread deforestation for crop and pasture lands. These slopes near Tenancingo have been totally cleared for grazing.

Land outside the large estates is cultivated wherever possible, no matter how small or inaccessible the plot.

Land scarcity also promotes intensive land use. Five crops are being cultivated in this one-manzana (0.7 hectare) family farm. Corn is planted in rows to the left of the eroded gully. The lower half of the maize area was hoed for weeds shortly before this photograph was taken. To the right of the gully are beans (top half) and rice (on the moist, lower slope). Just to the right of the rice are four rows of henequen, cultivated to supplement family income. The gully itself is planted in sorghum—the grain that gives the highest yields in the thin and rocky soils. The picture was taken in early August during the rainy season. From October to May this land to too dry to cultivate anything.

Land scarcity has forced peasants to plant maize even in the crevices of rock outcroppings.

Except for the construction of primary schools in several of the cantones, the rural areas show little evidence of modern change. In contrast to the clay-tile uniformity of the village, the countryside has a large number of *chozas,* or huts of straw thatch (these accounted for 35.4 percent of the 1,585 rural homes in 1971). Most of the others are of wattle-and-daub construction with clay-tile roofs; only the most affluent rural families are able to afford white-washed adobe. Electricity is not available in the cantones. Neither is running water; all water for household use has to be fetched from streams and local springs, and is very scarce in the dry season.

The demographic history of Tenancingo reflects in microcosm the national trends discussed in Chapter Two. According to local tradition, the area was inhabited before the conquest by a Pipil group called the Michapas. The village dates back to this time, suggesting a sizable pre-Hispanic population. But as elsewhere after the conquest, the population declined in the early colonial period, and by 1576 the town was reduced to 48 Indian families with 404 persons (Cardona Lazo 1939: 183). Thereafter the population grew very slowly, to reach an estimated 1,780 in 1858 (López 1858: 116). Then, in the late nineteenth century, the rate of growth began to pick up, pushing the population to 3,242 by 1878 and 4,089 by 1892 (Barberena & Fonseca 1909–14: 5). Since then, the municipality's intercensal growth rates have increased and decreased along with the national averages, though consistently at a lower level, as shown in Table 3.2. Since there is no evidence that Tenancingo has had either lower birth rates or higher death rates than other rural areas in El Salvador, this trend suggests that there has been a net out-migration from the area.

Two aspects of the region's economic history have particular relevance to this study. The first concerns the rise and fall of indigo cultivation, a major factor in the local land tenure patterns and community structure. According to local tradition, the Spanish settlement of the area began with the expansion of indigo cultivation to the north and east of San Salvador in the seventeenth century. One of the first Spaniards to arrive judiciously arranged a marriage between his daughter and Tenancingo's cacique. This not only ensured the Indians' acceptance of Spanish land claims, but also began the process of their acculturation. Descendants of the cacique and his Spanish wife became prominent citizens of the newly reorganized colonial village.

Nevertheless, Spanish indigo producers continued to encroach on Tenancingo lands, eventually forcing the Indians to appeal to the colonial government. As the local story has it, early in the eighteenth century, when the widow of a Spanish don sought to expand her indigo estate (which lay north of Tenancingo near Suchitoto), the Indians vigorously protested—first to the Alcalde Mayor of San Salvador and then to the Capitán General in Guatemala. Although they lost the contested land to the widow in public auction, some of it was regained when the Capitán General received their appeal. He decreed that a

T A B L E 3.2 *Population of Tenancingo, 1892–1971*

| Year | Population | Average annual growth rate in the interval | | Implied annual rate of migration |
		Tenancingo	National	
1892	4,089			
1930	5,434	0.71%	1.90%	−1.19%
1950	6,122	0.60	1.30	−0.70
1961	7,251	1.56	2.81	−1.25
1971	10,030	3.25	3.49	−0.24

SOURCE: Barberena 1892; ESDGEC 1942, 1953, 1965, 1974a.

portion of the widow's property should be returned to the Indians as an ejido. This same widow was apparently involved in another dispute with the Indian community of San Pedro Perulapán, 15 kilometers south of Tenancingo (D. Browning 1971: 91–94).

In the end, however, as in other parts of the Spanish colonial empire, the Indians' land tenure system and ultimately their cultural identity gave way under the impact of Spanish settlement. At the time of the indigo boom, the influx of Spanish families contributed directly to the disintegration of what remained of the Indians' protective corporate structure. By the time of the Liberal Reforms of the nineteenth century, this had probably disappeared altogether. Even before the last five caballerías (225 hectares) of ejidal lands were sold in 1882, the local population was described as less than one-quarter Indian (López 1858: 126). By then, a great number of the area's residents had not only been assimilated culturally, but had also been turned into landless laborers, employed on several indigo haciendas, a cattle estate, and a medium-sized farm producing sugarcane.

The ubiquity of individually operated small farms in the area today, in turn, is directly traceable to the collapse of the indigo market in the late nineteenth century. Several prominent landowning families left Tenancingo at that time, presumably headed for coffee-growing areas elsewhere in the country. Their vacated estates were then subdivided and sold to former workers and other local residents. One old hacienda site now appears to have been entirely converted to small farms. Evidence of this process of subdivision lies in the ruins of the indigo *obrajes* (processing mills) that can be seen today on many small farms. In short, the decline of indigo production resulted in a gradual return to food-crop production and to self-provisioning agriculture on small plots.

The second aspect of local history of importance to this study is the manufacture of "palm" hats, an industry that dates back to the colonial period and that still engages many households today. These hats are made of fronds of *Carludovica* sp. (family Cyclanthaceae), which are collected in the coastal swamps of the department of La Paz and brought to Tenancingo, to be dried and bleached in the sun, then split into long strands and braided. Several braids (*trenzas*) are then coiled and sewn together, and the hat is given final shape by a steam pressing.

Tenancingo was already well known for its hand-sewn hats in the mid-nineteenth century (López 1858: 26). Informants claim that the flourishing cottage industry was stimulated by the indigo trade, for the pack-mule teams carried hats as well as indigo to Guatemala and Honduras. Until the early 1890's when the sewing machine was introduced, hats were made in nearly every household. By 1928, however, the production from several treadle machines had replaced hand assembly throughout the region. The industry fell off for a time during World War II, when it proved to be more profitable simply to send the trenzas themselves to hat factories in Texas (whose normal supplies from the Philippines had been cut off). Then, in 1950, the first small-scale factory was established, with power sewing machines and semi-automated hat presses. By 1975, there were three such factories, which had virtually eliminated the shops relying on treadle machines.

The factories, however, do only the finishing work; the trenzas themselves are still hand-worked by women and children in peasant households throughout the area. Although their value has sharply declined in recent years, due in part to the competition of hats made from plastics and synthetic fibers, trenzas remain a major source of cash income for the poorest families in the area. Braiding as fast as possible and working every minute free from chores and meals, a woman can produce two dozen full-sized trenzas in one week. Most women produce one to one-and-a-half dozen a week, though the total number sold is often doubled by the work of their children. The income from the sale of trenzas (which in 1975 fetched about U.S. $1.75 per dozen) is often more than half the cash a poor rural family sees.

From this description, it is clear that Tenancingo is an "open peasant community" in the sense of the term as defined by Eric Wolf (1955) and used by Peggy Barlett (1975) for Costa Rica. Despite problems with this terminology elsewhere in the world (see Skinner 1971 on China), in Central America one can make a valid distinction between peasant communities that limit their membership, restrict their outside contacts, and regulate their members' rights to land and other possessions, and peasant communities with open membership, continuous interaction with the outside, and little regulation on the accumulation of wealth.

Today in Tenancingo there is no discernible vestige of any protective corporate structure. The population consists primarily of nuclear families living on or near plots of land that they own, rent, or share-crop. These plots of land are worked individually by adult males and their sons, with the occasional assistance of other male relatives in an extended household situation. The inhabitants all speak Spanish, they all wear Western manufactured clothing, and they retain no public ritual observance that can be traced to pre-Hispanic custom.

The agricultural landscape of Tenancingo reflects this absence of a closed community structure. The predominance of individually oper-ated small farms gives the countryside an erratic and highly frag-mented geometry. The plots are generally very small; indeed, a ma-jority fit the description of *microfinca* (less than 1.0 hectare) or *minifundio subfamiliar* (1.0–10.0 hectares) used by CEPAL 1973. Today there is only one landholding large enough to be called a haci-enda by the local residents, and holdings in the medium range are confined to a handful of commercial farms. The settlement pattern is predominantly a linear arrangement of houses sited along paths and trails, not one of kin clusters or residence groups. In general, clumps of houses occur only where major paths intersect.

Tenancingo has long been involved in regular economic interactions with the outside because of the hatmaking industry and the indigo trade. Today, larger farms in the area produce cattle, oranges, eggs, and some tobacco for sale in San Salvador. In addition, some of the smaller farms manage to produce a marketable surplus of basic food crops or grow minor cash crops to supplement the family's income. The "subsistence farmers" found in Tenancingo appear to be bound not by traditional orientations, but by a land base so small that it constrains their participation in cash-crop production.

Survey Results

Before I present the results of my survey, it is appropriate to say a few words about the procedures I used and about the sample popula-tion as a whole. As noted at the beginning of the chapter, statistical data for this analysis were collected in structured interviews with sam-ple families. Earlier village studies in El Salvador (e.g., Marroquín 1962, 1974) suggested that my best chance of obtaining accurate de-mographic information, particularly during busy agricultural periods, was to interview the women rather than the men. I designed my questionnaire accordingly, following the example of Stys 1957a and 1957b; Weiner & Lourie 1969; and the national fertility survey of the Asociación Demográfica Salvadoreña (1974). The questionnaire asked each woman for information on (1) her own life history and that of her current spouse; (2) the life history of all brothers and sisters of whom she had any knowledge; (3) the births, deaths, and economic activity of any children; and (4) the size, kind, and history of all family farm plots, including the form of tenure (owned, rented, sharecropped, etc.) and the number of years each plot had been used.*

The survey was conducted in the rainy-season months of August and September 1975, with the aid of six research assistants (all of whom had previous interviewing experience). We interviewed the women in their own residences and covered eight of the ten cantones surrounding the village. Two cantones were inaccessible because of rain-swollen rivers and had to be excluded. Interview households were chosen on the basis of a hamlet-stratified random sampling procedure, using house numbers supplied by the National Malaria Eradication program (Campaña Nacional Anti-Palúdica, or CNAP). Fortunately, we had detailed CNAP sketch maps for six of the cantones in our sample, giving the location of all residences. Maps for the other two were drawn by canvassing the areas and following the CNAP numbering procedure.

For appropriate controls in the analysis of mortality and migration data by farm size, a total sample of at least 250 cases was necessary. In addition, I felt the sample should be limited to women aged 25 to 55 so as to reduce the chances of memory error on the part of older women and to ensure that most of the women interviewed had at least begun to have families of their own. All told, we made 540 household visits (out of a total of 1,166 houses in the study area), which produced 285 completed questionnaires. Only 11 of the 255 eliminations (2 percent of the visits) were due to a refusal to be interviewed. In the other cases the women were either not home when we visited the house (on two separate occasions) or not of the appropriate age.

On my return to the United States, I coded, keypunched, and computer-analyzed the data, using the University of Michigan terminal system and the statistical analysis programs of MIDAS (Fox & Guire

* For an English translation of the questionnaire, see Appendix B.

1976). For the final analysis the sample was further refined to 258 cases, with the deletion of all families whose primary source of income was not agriculture or whose residence in Tenancingo was less than ten years.

Several characteristics of the study population are worth noting at the start as background information for the subsequent analyses. First, with respect to housing, 33.4 percent of the families live in palm-thatched huts, or chozas (a figure very close to the 1971 census total of 35.4 percent cited above), and most of the rest (64.5 percent) live in tile-roofed houses of wattle-and-daub or adobe-wall construction. A small fraction (2.1 percent) live in more "modern" cinder-block houses; all of these are located on the 12-kilometer stretch of road leading to the highway. Only 37 of the women interviewed (14.3 percent) were born outside the municipality, and all but six of these were born in neighboring rural areas. It is safe to conclude that there is little permanent in-migration of women into the area. On the other hand, 22.5 percent of the women born in Tenancingo no longer live in their natal hamlet; on the average they had moved four kilometers, generally to take up residence in the hamlet where their spouses were born. It should also be noted that 53.9 percent of the respondents say they can neither read nor write, compared with a figure of 51.2 percent for their spouses. Moreover, only 22 women (8.5 percent) reported attending school beyond the third grade.

Most of the women are either legally married to the present spouse in a church ceremony (56.6 percent) or *acompañada* (married by a common-law arrangement; 27.5 percent). Seven percent are separated, nearly all of them from common-law spouses. The rest of the group are nearly half and half widowed or single (4.3 percent and 4.7 percent, respectively). The median age at the time of marriage to current spouses, including both forms of union, is 21 years for the women and 26 years for the men. Slightly more than a fifth of the women (20.3 percent) claim to have had children by more than one man; this is generally confirmed by the last names of the children. The average age of the respondents is 36.4 years. To check the representativeness of the sample, I compared the age distribution of the respondents with the 1971 census figures for all rural women aged 25 to 49 in the municipality (ESDGEC 1974a: 59). That comparison revealed a maximum discrepancy of 8.4 percentage points (the sample was low for the 35–39 age group), and the chi-square test was insignificant at the 0.01 level. The sample can therefore be considered representative of the rural female population with respect to age.

Demographic Changes Between Generations

Figure 3.2 summarizes my findings on the numbers of children born, deceased before the age of 16, and surviving for both the present generation (respondents) and the past generation (their mothers). Breaking the figures down by sets of birth cohorts, we see that in the oldest set, 1900–1930, the number of births is both high (averaging 8.17 over the period) and fairly uniform. Child mortality is also high, averaging 2.61 children per woman, or roughly 31.9 percent of all reported births. The difference between these two figures—the average completed family size—has a mean of 5.56, with little variation over the subsample. Analysis of the variance by cohort in these measures produced insignificant F-statistics in each case, suggesting that conditions in Tenancingo did not change drastically as these cohorts were growing up.

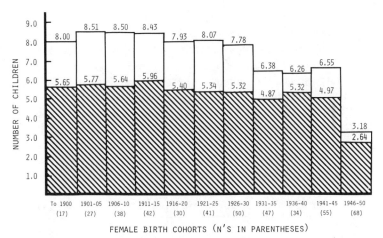

Fig. 3.2. Average numbers of births and surviving children by female birth cohorts in Tenancingo, 1890's–1950. The full histograms show the average number of births for each cohort; the open portion shows the average number of deaths of children under 16 years old; and the tone area shows the average number of surviving children. The fertility totals are complete only through the cohort of 1926–30.

Looking next at the cohorts of 1931–45, we find a considerable reduction in both the average number of births (6.42 per woman, against 8.17 for the earlier cohorts) and the average number of child deaths (1.40 against 2.61). But largely because of this reduced mortality, the family sizes of the two sets of cohorts (1890's–1930 and 1931–45) have changed very little. The mean for the younger set is 5.02, down slightly from 5.56 for the older. However, since some of these women are still of child-bearing age, we would expect the group's average to rise somewhat as they complete their fertile period.

To the extent that the total fertility rate has declined from 1930 to present, then, Figure 3.2 suggests that peasants have had fewer children simply to compensate for the decrease in child mortality, rather than with the idea of limiting the size of their families. As a further check on the lack of change in the completed family size between the generations, I compared the child births, deaths, and survivals for all the women aged 30–55 in the sample with the figures reported for their mothers. The results are given in Table 3.3. Generational changes in the total number of children born and deceased are statistically significant at the 0.01 level. The average number of surviving children, however, is not significantly different ($p > .05$). It may therefore be concluded that the peasant families of today are about as large as their parents' families were. Because child mortality is nearly half what it was in those days, it has simply taken fewer total births to have the same number of survivors.

Not surprisingly, the youngest cohort of women, aged only 25 to 30, does have smaller families. Of an average of 3.18 children born, 2.64 are still living. As might be expected, these figures are significantly different from the other cohorts ($p < .05$).

TABLE 3.3 *Demographic Changes Between Generations in Tenancingo*

Average number of children per woman	Past generation[a]	Present generation[b]	t-statistic	Significance
Born	8.35	6.72	5.37	$p < .01$
Deceased	2.80	1.62	2.94	$p < .01$
Surviving	5.55	5.10	1.87	n.s.

[a] Mothers of respondents.
[b] 188 respondents in the 30–55 age group.

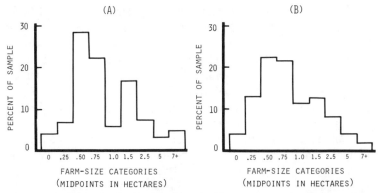

Fig. 3.3. Changes in the distribution of farmland between generations in Tenancingo. Diagram A shows the past generation's access to land (fathers of respondents; N = 191), and Diagram B shows the present generation's access to land (respondents themselves, in 1975; N = 236). The figures are based on data for all farm plots, regardless of tenure.

Changes in the Land Base Between Generations

The present-generation families (sample population) have access to less land than the past generation (respondents' fathers), both in terms of the total land available to them and in terms of landownership. The changes in the availability of land between generations are shown in Figure 3.3.* In the present generation, families have access to between 0 and 10 hectares, with an average of 1.10 hectares, compared with a range of 0 to 18 hectares and an average of 1.43 for the past generation. For the 177 cases for which data are complete for both generations, a

---

* The data on farm sizes were obtained from the interviews with female respondents. The figures were confirmed when possible with their spouses and, in a small subsample, with direct measurement. As a further check on the land areas used here, I compared the size distribution of plots in the sample with the distribution of plots in catastral photographs of the municipality provided by the Instituto Geográfico Nacional. Although it was not possible to verify individual landholdings, a chi-square test revealed no significant differences between the distributions.

For the analysis of land availability in this chapter, farm sizes have been converted from local units (*tareas, medios,* and *manzanas*) to hectares. The hectare areas have been grouped into size classes by approximate mid-points as follows: for the 0.01–0.34 range in hectares, 0.25 hectare; for the 0.35–0.62 range, 0.50; for the 0.63–0.90 range, 0.75; for the 0.91–1.18 range, 1.00; for the 1.19–1.74 range, 1.50; for the 1.75–3.49 range, 2.50; for the 3.50–6.99 range, 5.0; and for the ≥7.00 range, 7.00+.

Student *t*-test reveals that the difference between the means—1.06 for the present generation and 1.48 for the past—is significant at the 0.05 level.

Just as the overall land base has shrunk between the generations, so has the average size of the family-owned farm. Among the 111 fathers who are reported to have owned land, the average holding was 2.12 hectares. The average for the 112 landowning families of the present generation is only 1.60 hectares.

Looking strictly at the local level, and ignoring for the moment the national context, we can attribute both of these trends to large family sizes and local population growth. Consider, for example, how the land has been fragmented in just two generations through inheritance. Some 15 percent of the respondents (39 women) have inherited land from their parents, in most cases, from their fathers. In every instance they have received only a fraction of their parent's holding, sharing their inheritance with some or all of those of their siblings who have remained in the area. The same applies to the respondents' spouses. Of the 61 men who have inherited land (again primarily from their fathers), only nine received a plot as large as that farmed by their parents. In the other 52 cases the family farm had again been divided among two or more of the surviving offspring. Obviously such a process, if it continues, means smaller and smaller farms for each successive generation.

The property-owning families account for only 43.4 percent of the sample population. Most of the others—89 families (34.5 percent of the total)—are tenants, i.e., either renters or sharecroppers. Their plots are smaller in general than the owned farms, averaging 0.75 hectare, and their tenure is relatively unstable. Rental and sharecropping agreements are usually made on a year-to-year basis at the discretion of the landowner, and they tend not to be renewed. The median tenure period for rented and sharecropped plots is one year, compared with nine years for owned property. Thirty of the 112 property-owning families are also tenants, renting or sharecropping an average of 0.67 hectare to supplement 0.46 hectare of property. In this case, too, the owned plots are held much longer than the others—a median of eight years, compared with two. In the analyses described below, these 30 families are treated as landowners.

The other non-propertied families fall into three groups. Thirty-four of them (13.2 percent of the sample) farm land lent to them without charge by relatives. Because of the relative stability of these holdings (median tenure is six years), this land is treated as property in my subsequent analyses. Another 13 families live as colonos on larger farms, working the owner's land in exchange for the use of small parcels for their own purposes. Finally, ten families (3.9 percent of the total) are landless and depend wholly on a cash income derived from the women's production of trenzas and the men's work as agricultural laborers, or *jornaleros* (often accompanied by one or more male children). In addition, 21 men with small rented or owned plots work six months or more per year as jornaleros, and 30 others do day work occasionally.

Although the land base of the present-generation families is small, it does show signs of increasing slightly in the course of the family cycle. Among the 135 peasant families that have farmed for at least ten years, for example, the average land used increased from 0.98 hectare per family in 1965 to 1.22 hectares in 1975 ($t = 3.40, p < .05$). Much of this increase is due to inheritances in later years and to rentals begun when the sons became old enough to help their fathers. In most families this help is expected by age ten.

Family Income

Because of the long history of trenza manufacture in the area and a price squeeze on palm fronds, the respondents keep careful account of their family's cash income. Figure 3.4 shows the distribution of the average monthly income for the 258 sample families. The distribution

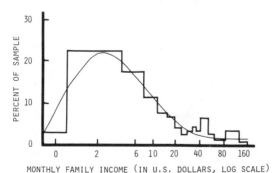

Fig. 3.4. Monthly family income in Tenancingo. Based on data for the full sample population ($N = 258$).

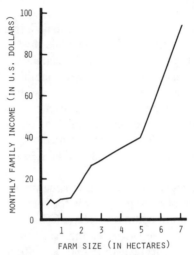

Fig. 3.5. Relationship between monthly family income and land base in Tenancingo. Based on data for the families in which the men work only on the family plot (N = 92).

approximates a log-normal frequency curve, with a median family income of U.S. $8.00 to $12.00 per month. Only seven families have no cash income, which is not especially surprising, considering the ubiquity of the trenza braiding. For most of the 22.5 percent of families that earn $4.00 or less per month, the sole source of cash income is the sale of trenzas.

Figure 3.5 shows the nearly exponential relationship between average monthly family income and land availability for the subset of 92 families in which the men work only on the family plot. As we see, the average monthly income increases from $8.00 to $10.00 for families with farms of 1.5 hectares or less to $94.00 for those with farms of 7.0 hectares or more. The minimum incomes are almost exclusively derived from the production of trenzas; the maximum ones almost exclusively from the sale of agricultural products, notably cattle, oranges, and tobacco. Among the families with farms of 1.5 hectares or less, 97 percent claim that they need all of their annual harvest for food. Aggregate rural family income gradients by farm size similar to these have been reported by CEPAL 1971, ESMAG 1973, Burke 1976, and Colindres 1976.

Relationship Between Child Mortality and Farm Size

In Chapter One I proposed that access to land strongly influences the ability of Salvadorean peasants to survive and reproduce. This section provides a statistical test of that hypothesis for the two generations of Tenancingo families, using child mortality figures as an indicator.

The general relationship between land use and child mortality for the past generation is shown in Figure 3.6. The curves represent the percent of all children born to respondents' mothers who died before reaching reproductive age (under 16) by farm-size category and tenure. They are based on data for 1,326 births from 154 families, a subsample that omits all families where the major source of livelihood was not agriculture and where the respondent was the last child born. (These women were excluded because preliminary analysis revealed that they recalled significantly fewer instances of mortality among their siblings—an average of 1.43—compared with women of other birth orders—an average of 2.60.)

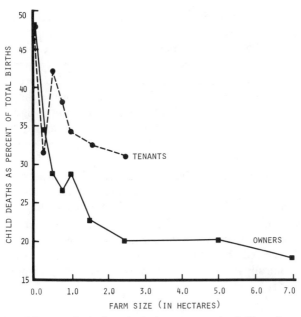

Fig. 3.6. Child mortality by farm size in the past generation in Tenancingo.

T A B L E 3.4   *Child Mortality by Farm Size in the Past Generation in Tenancingo*

Farm size in hectares[a]	Number of families	Average number of children per family			Average rate of mortality[b]
		Born	Deceased	Surviving	
0.00	69[c]	9.61	3.38	6.23	33.3%
0.25	7	9.37	3.29	6.08	27.3
0.50	16	8.88	2.56	6.31	25.6
0.75	19	7.79	2.05	5.74	22.6
1.00	6	7.00	2.00	5.00	26.2
1.50	16	7.19	1.63	5.56	21.1
2.50	6	8.00	1.67	6.33	19.9
3.50+	15	7.93	1.53	6.40	17.0
TOTAL/AVERAGE	154	8.61	2.60	6.01	27.3%
F-statistic		2.64	2.46	0.92	2.06
Significance		$p < .05$	$p < .05$	n.s.	$p < .05$

[a] Farm-size categories by midpoints.

[b] Number of children deceased divided by number born by individual family and then averaged over all families in a given farm-size category.

[c] Includes tenants (renters and sharecroppers).

As we see, the percentage of child deaths declines rapidly from 48 percent among landless families to a plateau of about 20 percent for families owning 2.5 hectares or more. The overall average for owners is 26.2 percent. Child mortality among tenant families is appreciably higher, except for an apparently anomalous total of 31.5 percent for the group in the 0.25-hectare class. The overall average for the tenant families is 36.9 percent. Note that the percentages in the figure are computed from the total number of children born and deceased among all families of a given farm size and tenure type. The figure therefore ignores within-group variability.

In order to see if that variability could affect these results, I conducted a one-way analysis of variance in mortality according to the amount of land owned by each family. Tenant farmers with no owned land were included in the 0-size class. The results of this analysis are shown in Table 3.4. Consider first column 3, which shows the average number of deceased children per woman. The number decreases almost monotonically from 3.38 among tenants and landless families to

1.53 among owners of 5.0 hectares or more. These differences were found to be statistically significant. Looking next at the fourth column, the numbers of children who survived to adulthood, we find that there was no significant variance among the groups. Indeed the average in the lowest farm-size class, 6.23, is very similar to the average in the highest, 6.40. (The low average rate of mortality in the 1.0-hectare class is probably a small-sample artifact.) In other words, completed family sizes are very similar over the range of farm sizes, despite the greater mortality at the low end.

As shown in column 2, families with little or no land of their own appear to "compensate" for their higher rate of child mortality by having more children; their average number of births is 9.61, compared with 7.93 for families with 3.5 hectares or more, or indeed 7.00 and 7.19 births for families in the 1.0-hectare and 1.5-hectare classes. These differences are significant at the 0.05 level. Unfortunately, the data do not reveal just what causes this compensatory trend in fertility. The most likely possibilities are (1) a hastened return to ovulation on the death of a newborn, (2) a more direct, voluntary form of compensation, or (3) a combination of the two. Whatever the case, the data do suggest that elevated mortality is a direct stimulus to high rates of fertility in the Tenancingo sample.

Finally, as shown in the last column, the average rate of mortality (calculated by individual families), is also related to farm size, decreasing by about one-half over the range, from 33 percent among tenants and the landless to 17 percent among families with 3.5 hectares or more. Despite some variance between families reflected in the F-statistic shown here, the overall trend shown in Figure 3.6 is confirmed by this analysis. The null hypothesis of no relationship between scarcity and survival can be rejected. According to the child mortality indicator for the past generation, the ability of peasants in Tenancingo to survive and reproduce is strongly influenced by their access to land.

A similar trend is shown for the present generation in Figure 3.7. The curves in this case are based on 1,109 births among 157 women in the 30–55 age group (a 30-year age limit was imposed as a means of reducing variability in the data due to families with children who are

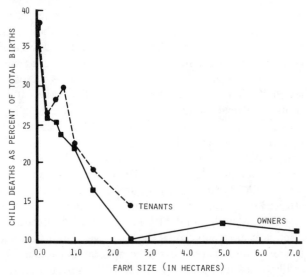

Fig. 3.7. Child mortality by farm size in the present generation in Tenancingo. The present generation covers only the 1920–45 female birth cohorts.

still very young). From a high of 38.5 percent among landless families, child mortality drops to a plateau of 10–12 percent among families that own 2.5 hectares or more. Compared with the past generation, the differences between tenants and owners are much diminished. An average of 27.4 percent of all children born to tenants had died by the time of the interview, against 36.9 percent for the past generation. Similarly, an average of 21.0 percent of the children born to landowners had died, against the past generation's 26.2 percent. Again these data are computed from the total births and deaths for each farm-size category and thus ignore within-group variability.

Figure 3.8 compares the child mortality among the landowning families for the two generations. As we can clearly see, the relationship between land scarcity and survival is qualitatively similar for both generations, although deflected to lower levels in the present one. Moreover, the figure indicates that the decline in mortality rates be-

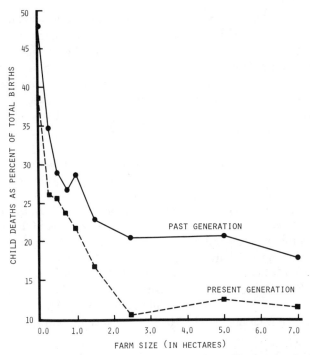

Fig. 3.8. Changes in child mortality between generations of landowning families in Tenancingo.

tween the generations is most pronounced among families with large farms. For example, the mortality rate decreased substantially, from 20.8 percent to 10.2 percent, among families in the 2.5-hectare class, but fell only slightly among those in the 0.5-hectare class, from 28.9 percent to 25.4 percent. This finding suggests that improvements in rural health care and sanitation in the past 50 years are not equally available to all families in the area. Cash income (Fig. 3.5) is surely one factor that restricts the access of the landless and land-poor to medicine.

Again I checked to see if within-group variability affects the mortality trends. Because of the confounding effect of the ages of the present-generation women, many of whom are still in their child-bearing years, the within-group variability here was much greater. To reduce that variability, I imposed two conditions before analyzing the variance. First, I limited the families in the analysis to those that have had a total of at least four children (the 30-to-55 age requirement was dropped). Second, I grouped the families into broader farm-size categories: 0 hectares (including renters), 0.01–0.90 hectares, 0.91–3.49 hectares, and 3.50 hectares or more. The results are shown in Table 3.5.

Looking again at the figures on the average number of deceased children, we see that the number decreases monotonically, from 1.83 in the 0-hectare category to 1.10 among owners with 3.5 hectares or more. Further, landless and colono families have lost an average of 2.04 children. Although these differences are suggestive of the pattern seen in the past generation, they are not statistically significant because of high within-group variance ($F = 1.81$). There is, however, significant variation in the average number of surviving children between farm-size categories, with families in the smallest size category having an average of 5.30 living children, compared with a maximum of 6.72 among families with 0.91–3.49 hectares. In contrast to the past

T A B L E 3.5   *Child Mortality by Farm Size in the Present Generation in Tenancingo*

Farm size in hectares	Number of families	Average number of children per family			Average rate of mortality[a]
		Born	Deceased	Surviving	
0.00[b]	92 (23)	7.13 (7.43)	1.83 (2.04)	5.30 (5.39)	23.5 (25.5)%
0.01–0.90	44	7.11	1.80	5.32	24.5
0.91–3.49	25	7.84	1.12	6.72	12.7
3.50+	10	7.30	1.10	6.20	13.6
TOTAL/AVERAGE	171	7.24	1.67	5.57	21.6%
F-statistic		0.64	1.81	4.36	3.55
Significance		n.s.	n.s.	p < .05	p < .05

[a] Number of children deceased divided by number born by individual family and then averaged over all families in a given farm-size category.

[b] The first figure includes tenants (renters and sharecroppers), as well as colonos and the landless. The figure in parenthesis excludes tenants.

T A B L E 3.6   *Regression Analysis of Child Mortality in the Past and Present*
Generations of the Tenancingo Sample

Source of mortality data	Constant		Total number of births, B, in family		Natural-logged land area, L, used by family	
	Regression coefficient	Statistic	Regression coefficient	Statistic	Regression coefficient	Statistic
Past generation						
(N = 191)[a]	−1.06(*C'*)		0.49(*C''*)		−0.28(*C'''*)	
Standard error		0.41		0.04		0.08
t-statistic		−2.57		11.65		−3.41
Significance		0.05		0.001		0.001
Partial correlation		—		0.65		−0.24
Present generation						
(N = 236)[b]	0.02(*C'*)		0.36(*C''*)		−0.37(*C'''*)	
Standard error		0.21		0.02		0.07
t-statistic		0.10		14.72		−5.09
Significance		n.s.		0.0001		0.0001
Partial correlation		—		0.69		−0.32

NOTE: The regression model predicts the number of child deaths, D, in a family according to the formula $D = C' + C'' (B) + C''' (L)$.

[a] $R^2 = 0.48$. Multiple R = 0.69. F-statistic = 86.6. p < .0001.
[b] $R^2 = 0.49$. Multiple R = 0.70. F-statistic = 112.6. p < .0001.

generation, then, there does not appear to be a mortality-compensating fertility differential in these families. That inference is supported by a variance test of the total numbers of children born, which reveals no significant differences among farm-size categories. However, these results cannot be taken at face value, since the confounding effect of female age has not been completely controlled in this instance. As we saw in the previous section, as time goes on families do tend to acquire more land and to have more children. If the women in the smaller farm-size categories are substantially younger than their counterparts on larger farms, these results could be spurious. That is, in fact, exactly what one finds. In these same families and farm-size categories, the average age of the women increases in the predicted direction: 36.1 years in the 0-hectare category, 37.9 in the 0.91–3.49 category, and 43.2 years in the 3.50 and over category. The F-statistic in this case is

5.80, significant at the 0.001 level. It is therefore likely that the positive association between numbers of surviving children and farm size in the present generation is an artifact of the age distribution.

As shown in the last column of Table 3.5, the relationship between the average rate of mortality and farm size is significant at the 0.05 level. Average mortality decreases from 23.5 percent in the smallest farm-size class to 13.6 percent in the largest. This result accords with our finding for the past generation; but it, too, might be confounded by the female-age effect.

To eliminate most of that effect from the present generation's analysis and also to provide a comparative summary of the relationship between land availability and mortality for both generations, I conducted a least-squares regression analysis on data from each generation. Because the overall mortality curves of Figures 3.7 and 3.8 suggested an exponential mortality decrease with land, I used the natural log of the family farm area as the land-base independent variable (to prevent negative log values, all areas were multiplied by ten before the log transformation, and 0 land was treated as 0.1 hectare). In addition, to control for the female-age effect, a second independent variable was included—the total number of children born in a family, which is highly correlated with female age. An extremely simple log-linear regression model was then fitted to each data set:

$$D = C' + C''(B) + C'''(L),$$

where D is the predicted number of child deaths in a family, B is the total number of children born in the family, L is the natural-logged land area used by the family, regardless of tenure, and C', C'', and C''' are the coefficient values determined by the least-squares method. The model is obviously not designed to explain as much mortality variance as would be possible with the set of survey data collected. Rather it attempts to see just how much of the variance can be explained by the two key variables identified in the preceding analyses. If it is true that the mortality differential between generations is most pronounced among the larger farm-size categories, we would expect C''' to have a larger negative value for the present generation than for the past.

The results of the regression analysis are shown in Table 3.6. The table gives log-linear regression models for both generations, together with R^2 values, F-statistics, partial correlation coefficients, and tests of significance. It reveals two important findings. First, these simple models explain nearly one-half (48 percent and 49 percent) of all variance in child deaths among families in the sample. This confirms the important influence of the two independent variables on child mortality. Second, the results, as expected, show a greater negative coefficient C''' for the present generation than for the past. This result is particularly important in light of the lower value of C'' for the present generation. In other words, although overall mortality is reduced in the present generation (i.e., fewer deaths per births), the effect of the land base is even more pronounced now than in the past. These results are therefore a solid demonstration not only that the ability of peasants to survive and reproduce is directly related to their access to land, but also that the scarcity of land in Tenancingo has an even stronger impact on the child mortality rates in the present generation than in the past.

Relationship Between Out-Migration and Farm Size

The second major hypothesis to be tested on data from Tenancingo is that the frequency (or probability) of rural out-migration is directly proportional to the scarcity of land. That is, can it be shown that the difficulties of survival that stem from a small and dwindling land base provide an important motivation for rural people to migrate to other rural areas, to urban centers, or to Honduras?

This hypothesis can be tested by analyzing the data on the permanent out-migration of brothers and sisters of the respondents (i.e., surviving children of the past generation) as a function of the land worked by their fathers. For simplicity and to minimize variance, this analysis focuses on the relationship between (1) the percentage of brothers and sisters who have permanently left the hamlet where they were born and (2) the amount of land owned by their father. As further controls on the data, the analysis is based on 162 complete cases where both parents had reached at least the age of 45 and where the family had been primarily dependent on agriculture for its livelihood.

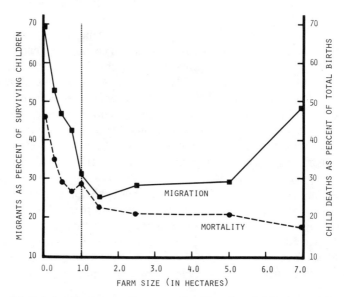

Fig. 3.9. Relationship Between Permanent Out-Migration of Offspring and Size of Parents' Landholdings in Tenancingo.

In these families, data are complete for 955 surviving siblings, of whom 350 (36.6 percent) have left their Tenancingo birthplace.*

Figure 3.9 shows the frequency of permanent out-migration for all siblings in this sample by the size of the farm owned by their parents. From a high of 69.2 percent among completely landless families, the percentage of out-migrants drops to a plateau of 25–29 percent for

---

* For almost three-quarters of these people, the move from their native hamlet was truly a migration out of the area and not simply a relocation to a nearby hamlet. But I should say here that the information on the destinations of this migrant group is less complete than I could have wished. In 300 cases respondents were unable to say what had become of a brother or sister; generally these were siblings who had moved away many years before and never returned to visit. The sketchiness of the information is particularly problematical for estimating the extent of the migration out of El Salvador. I have been able to identify only 11 migrants (3.1 percent) as definitely residing in Honduras at the time of the interview. Another 11 were reported to be in other countries, six in Guatemala and five in the United States. However, many of the 300 mi-

farms in the 1.5-hectare to 5.0-hectare classes. The percentage then increases to 48.1 among the children of landowners with 7.0 or more hectares of farmland. For comparison, the figure also includes the mortality curve among the children of this generation, from Figure 3.8. Apart from the largest farm-size category, the two curves are closely parallel. Both decrease rapidly from their highest value among landless families to plateaus that begin with the same size class, 1.5 hectares. Moreover, it should be noted that a full 78.3 percent of all the out-migrants (274 of the 350) came from families that owned 1.0 hectare of farmland or less (i.e., up to the dotted line in the figure). In other words, more than three-quarters of all the migrants from a random sample of families in this community of small farmers came from the excluded population of landless and land-poor. These two findings—the parallel nature of the frequency curves and the observation that most migrants are from landless and land-poor families—suggest that migration does indeed occur in proportion to the life-and-death consequences of land scarcity.

The exception to the general trend is not particularly surprising. Unlike their less fortunate neighbors, the children of the larger farm households have not been "pushed" off the land; this group has instead been "pulled" toward the educational and career opportunities of San Salvador. More than three-quarters of the migrants from the largest farm-size class (20 of 26) reside in San Salvador, where a majority attended high schools and trade or secretarial schools. These opportunities were generally not available to the children of the poorer peasants.

As a test of the significance of the variation in migration frequencies

---

grants whose whereabouts were unknown, and who are therefore not included in the 955 cases analyzed here, probably moved out of the country. A reliable male informant, for example, who was expelled from Honduras in 1969, estimates that some 200 of his fellows from the Quezalapa valley (Tenancingo and neighboring Cinquera) were expelled with him.

Another problem in these data may be a bias from the selective out-migration of whole families. Although data were not collected about former residents of the hamlets, it is likely that the frequency of whole-family departures varies as a function of landholdings in a pattern similar to the sibling migration described below. The migration frequencies described here are therefore likely to be conservative.

between farm-size categories, I again subjected the data to an analysis of variance. Because of substantial variance within the size classes due to other factors, the calculated F-statistic of 1.37 is not significant (p = .21). The variance is comparatively high in the 0.25–0.74-hectare classes, suggesting that migration differentials are not very sensitive to these small differences in the land base. I therefore decided to lump all the groups with less than a hectare of land and compare them, using a t-test, to a 1.0–5.0-hectare group. The mean number of migrants per family in the under-one-hectare group is 2.63, significantly different from 1.79 for the larger group (t = 2.04, p < .05). Moreover, an average of 47.4 percent of the land-poor group has migrated, compared with 30.2 for the other group. This difference is also statistically significant (t = 2.51, p < .05). It can therefore be concluded that (1) migration tendencies are not quite as sensitive to small differences in the land base as child mortality rates, but (2) the variance between suitably lumped categories remains statistically significant. The null hypothesis can therefore be rejected in favor of the alternative hypothesis proposed here.

In looking at the destination of the 350 migrants whose movements can be ascertained, one finds several clear trends in the out-migration from Tenancingo. For example, the data show that these people have moved an average point-to-point map distance (as opposed to highway distance) of only 23.6 kilometers. Not surprisingly, San Salvador — just 30 kilometers away — is the most popular destination (attracting 127 of the migrants, or 36.3 percent). Another 29 live in the nearby city of Cojutepeque (where Tenancingo migrants form the core of a hat-making industry), and 39 others in various urban areas of the department of La Libertad, primarily the city of Santa Tecla. These three urban destinations account for 55.7 percent of all cases of out-migration and for virtually all of the sample's rural-urban migration.

Two principal areas of attraction are also evident in the rural-to-rural migration. Sixteen of the migrants are now living in the department of Santa Ana, the center of El Salvador's coffee production, and 21 have settled in the department of La Paz; most of this last group are involved in the palm trade with Tenancingo. In the remaining 96 cases (27.4 percent) the person has moved to a different hamlet in Tenancingo or to some nearby municipality.

Conclusions

The analysis of data from the survey sample of peasant families in Tenancingo provides direct support for two of my major hypotheses. First, the ability of peasants to survive and reproduce appears strongly influenced by their access to land. The child mortality figures indicate that the threat to survival and reproduction grows exponentially as the land base of families approaches zero, a result that was obtained for both of the generations in the survey. Log-linear regression analyses in both cases explained nearly half of all the variance in family mortality data. In addition, the sign and magnitude of the regression coefficients indicate that though overall child mortality has declined between generations, the relative influence of the land base is even more pronounced at present. This is primarily because the greatest decrease in mortality between generations occurred among the families with large farms.

To the best of my knowledge, this study is the first to demonstrate a direct link between peasant family demography and land use in Latin America. Indeed, there are surprisingly few studies that attempt to examine the ecological basis of fertility and child mortality in peasant families anywhere in the world. Perhaps the closest analogue is Wincenty Stys's "The Influence of Economic Conditions on the Fertility of Peasant Women" (1957a). His analysis, based on interviews with more than 4,900 peasant families in southern Poland in the 1940's, produced mortality patterns remarkably similar to those described here. The mortality differential among peasants' mothers (his past generation) ranged from 15.8 percent of the children born to families with 30–50 hectares to 25.9 percent in families with 0.0–0.5 hectare. Among peasants' wives (his present generation), child mortality ranged from 10.9 percent for families with 15–20 hectares to 14.9 percent among families with 0.0–0.5 hectare. Considering the differences in culture, social organization, and agriculture between Poland and El Salvador, the degree of similarity in these trends is striking. There are, however, important differences in the fertility patterns. In my study, a total fertility differential by farm size was found to be positively associated with the mortality differential in the families that have completed their childbearing. This suggests that parents with access to very small plots may somehow be compensating for the elevated mortality. Among Polish peasants, however, the total born on the largest farms (9.11 in the 30-to-50-hectare class) was nearly double the total born on the smallest (4.88 in the 0.0–0.5 class). It may be that Polish inheritance patterns act as a constraint on fertility among small farmholders, but this is a subject I must leave to a later study.

Two recent studies of malnutrition in Central America look at some possible intervening variables for the demographic analysis presented here. One of these studies, on Guatemala, analyzes the relationship between family land availability and the nutritional status of children in four rural villages (Valverde et al. 1977). Defining moderate malnutrition by standard measures (children who are below 75 percent of the normal weight for their age), the authors found that 38 percent of the children of farmers with 0.0–1.9 manzanas (0.0–1.3 hectares) were malnourished, compared with 17 percent in families with 5.0 manzanas or more (3.5 + hectares). These results are highly compatible with the mortality data presented here. In fact, the authors claim their information "implies substantial differences in mortality rates" (p. 6).

In the other study, on Costa Rica, access to land was found to be the primary variable affecting nutritional status in the rural community of Concepción de San Ramón (Rawson & Valverde 1976). A chi-square test revealed a statistically significant difference between the number of malnourished children from farms of less than 2.0 manzanas and the number from larger farms. The data further suggested certain "risk factors" associated with the smaller farm holdings. For example, in families with farms of less than 2.0 manzanas, the fathers tended to work as day laborers in addition to farming their own plots. A similar tendency exists in Tenancingo. The Costa Rican study showed that this outside employment was associated with a lower production of subsistence foods on the man's own plot, and that the family's diet was detrimentally affected in consequence, since the cash earnings were insufficient to meet the food needs. The mothers in these families were also likely to take outside jobs; and those who did so tended to have children with below normal weights, primarily because of improper care in their absences from the home (p. 15). Because most of the women in Tenancingo are able to work at the trenzas in their own homes, this factor may be less important there. Nevertheless, these findings may be taken as supportive evidence for the mortality trends described above.

The Tenancingo data also support a second hypothesis of this study—that the rural out-migration of Salvadorean peasants is largely in response to resource scarcity. As we have seen, the smaller the family land base, the greater the tendency among the siblings of the women we interviewed to move away from their birthplace. Out-migration tendencies are apparently related to the family land base in a nonlinear fashion. Indeed, there is a close connection between the migration percentages and the mortality rates by farm-size category, suggesting that migration has been a response to the survival and reproduction consequences of the land shortage. Despite some within-group variance, the association of migration patterns with the family resource base was statistically significant.

These findings corroborate a hypothesis concerning the process of rural-urban migration in Latin America that has previously been examined almost exclusively with aggregate data (e.g., Geisert 1963; Kosinski & Prothero 1970; Thomas 1971). That hypothesis, as succinctly summarized by R. P. Shaw, is "that motivation to migrate will be initiated by the emergence of noxious or unsatisfactory conditions in the rural sector."

Once migration is considered [by a rural dweller], information on rural-urban income and amenity differentials is expected to be actively sought as part of the decision whether or not to actually migrate. In other terms, rural "pushes" may operate both directly and indirectly in creating motivation to migrate, whereas urban "pulls" may operate largely as the "conditioners" of decisions on where to migrate. If so, this would help to explain why rural-urban migration flows persist in the fact of high rates of urban unemployment, serious urban housing shortages, and insignificant amenity differentials. (Shaw 1976: 52)

My data, however, suggest a further refinement of "push" and "pull" influences. The vast majority of Tenancingo's out-migrants (78.3 percent) came from families with little or no land, directly in proportion to an ecological definition of "push" factors. The only other large group of out-migrants were the children of the better-off families, those with landholdings of 7.0 hectares or more. The evidence suggests that the opportunities available in San Salvador for those who can afford the costs constitute an appreciable migration "pull."

A second hypothesis advanced by Shaw—that the incidence of rural out-migration is a product of interactions between population increase and the land tenure system of an area—is also supported by my data. Indeed, I believe that the methodology of study site selection and survey analysis I have employed provides the local-level equivalent of Shaw's elaborate statistical procedure to predict rural out-migration from aggregate data on population growth and land tenure (see Shaw 1976).

As we have seen, the scarcity of land in Tenancingo has certainly been affected by the growth of the population and by the large families of the agricultural residents. Considered purely at the local level, that scarcity may appear to be almost entirely a function of population growth (see H. Browning 1970). However, as we have also seen, the very existence of crowded peasant communities like Tenancingo in El Salvador can be explained by land tenure dynamics and competitive exclusion in other parts of the country. Thus, before leaping to the conclusion that mortality rates, migration patterns, or even the emergence of new agricultural methods is "the result of population pressure on fixed resources" (a mistake made by Barlett in her 1975 study of Costa Rican peasants, for example), one must first consider the dynamics of resource availability in a given community against the larger national context. The land scarcity observed in Tenancingo is clearly the product of both population growth and land concentration.

Finally, a word about the implications of this study for interpreting the ecological background to the conflict between El Salvador and Honduras. Because Tenancingo was carefully chosen as a representative example of the conditions facing small farmers in El Salvador, we can reasonably infer that the consequences of land scarcity there have been experienced elsewhere in the country. If so, we might also expect the responses of the campesinos in other areas to follow similar patterns. The evidence presented here strongly supports the hypothesis made in the preceding chapter that most of El Salvador's out-migrants have come from the ranks of the landless and the land-poor. Further, it suggests that such out-migration has occurred largely in response to resource scarcity at the local level.

Whereas previous explanations of the accelerating resource scarcity in El Salvador and the resulting out-migration have focused almost exclusively on the role of aggregate population growth, I have argued that distributional dynamics play a prominent role as well. The evidence I have presented here plainly indicates that above and beyond population growth, as time has passed increasing numbers of Salvadoreans have virtually been pushed off the land base of the country, impelling them to migrate either to urban areas or to more promising rural areas, including Honduras. In the next two chapters we will first take a closer look at the conditions Salvadorean migrants found in Honduras, and will then attempt to evaluate how those migrants affected land availability there.

CHAPTER FOUR

The Question of Resource Abundance in Honduras

At first inspection, the ecological conditions confronting the Honduran peasants appear to be far more favorable than those facing their Salvadorean counterparts. Not only does Honduras have more than five times the total land area of El Salvador (see Fig. 4.1), but also the average Honduran farm is almost twice as large as the average farm in El Salvador. Moreover, as we see in Table 4.1, in 1966, when Honduras's borders were still open to Salvadorean immigrants, less than one quarter of the land area was incorporated into farms, in contrast to three-quarters for El Salvador (in 1961).

In addition, Honduras's population has remained smaller than El Salvador's ever since the early colonial period. Figure 4.2 compares the population curves of the two countries over time. Though the curves share certain features—a sharp decrease following colonization, 300 years of stagnation during colonial rule, and a steadily increasing slope since the early 1800's—the figure shows two differences of importance to this study. One is the relatively greater severity of the impact of the Spanish conquest on Honduras. El Salvador's population, it will be recalled, fell to an estimated low of 50,000–60,000 in 1551; but by then Honduras's population, which had been roughly equal to El Salvador's in 1524, numbered less than 24,000 (the estimate for 1541), and it went on to dwindle to a mere 18,000 in 1590 (Johannessen 1963: 30). This greater decline can be attributed to the Spaniards' exploitation of Honduran Indians in the early years both as slaves for Panama and South America and as mineworkers within the country itself. Most of the remaining Indians saw their land converted to ranching and grazing, so that, as Johannessen puts it, "as the Indian population disappeared, livestock took its place" (p. 29).

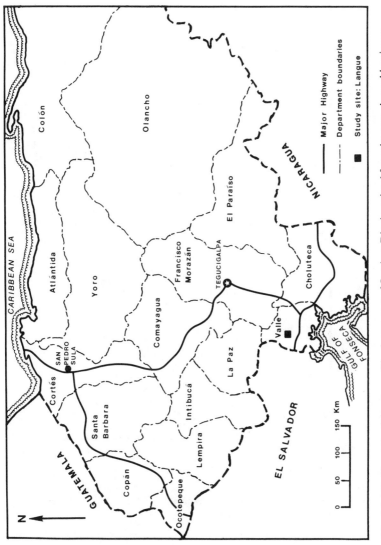

Fig. 4.1. The Republic of Honduras. The department of Gracias a Dios is omitted from the map. A roughly triangular expanse of 17,500 square kilometers of rainforest and swampland, it is largely uninhabited.

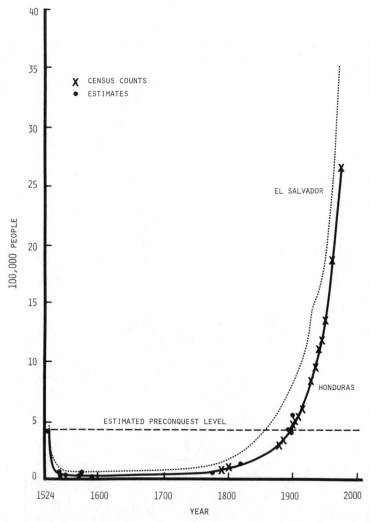

Fig. 4.2. Population growth of Honduras, 1524–1974. SOURCE: Johannessen 1963: 30; MacLeod 1973: 59; Pérez Brignoli 1973a; Molina Chocano 1975a; HDGEC 1977: 9. The El Salvador curve is from Fig. 2.1.

The other important difference in the population trends of the countries lies in their modern rates of growth. Honduras's rate of growth overtook El Salvador's in 1881, as shown in Table 4.2. After that, it remained consistently higher through 1961, although Honduras's total population was still only 75.1 percent of El Salvador's in that year. Part of the reason for the higher growth rates of Honduras in this period was the accelerating immigration of Salvadoreans, as discussed in Chapter Two (see Fig. 2.18 and Table 2.6). In the years of greatest immigration, 1950–60, the influx of Salvadoreans accounted for an estimated 22.6 percent of the total growth of the Honduran population.

Taken together, these land and population comparisons imply that as recently as 1961, El Salvador was still more than seven times more densely populated than Honduras. As described in Chapter One, this differential is a key element of the neo-Malthusian interpretation of the Soccer War. According to this view, Salvadorean peasants were lured away from the population pressures at home by the promise of idle lands and untapped resources in the relatively vast expanses of Honduras.

A closer examination of conditions in Honduras, however, reveals that life is not nearly so lush for its inhabitants as these figures might

T A B L E 4.1 *Comparison of the Land Bases of El Salvador and Honduras, 1960's*

Category	El Salvador (1961)	Honduras (1965–66)	Ratio Honduras to El Salvador
Land area: In square kilometers	21,040.78	112,088.00	5.33
Average farm size: In hectares	6.97	13.57	1.94
Land in farms: In square kilometers	15,814.28	24,196.08	1.53
As percent of total land	75.2%	21.6%	
Cropland:[a] In square kilometers	4,793.78	5,325.93	1.11
As percent of total land	22.8%	4.8%	

SOURCE: ESDGEC 1967; HDGEC 1968.
[a] Does not include fallow land.

T A B L E   4.2   *Population Growth of Honduras,*
1590–1974

Year	Estimated population on July 1	Average annual growth rate in the interval	Average annual growth rate of El Salvador in comparable periods
1590	36,000		
1778	88,100	0.48%	0.31%
1791	93,500	0.46	1.07
1881	307,300	1.33	1.42
1895	395,600	1.82	1.71
1930	854,200	2.22	1.90
1950	1,369,700	2.39	1.30
1961	1,895,800	3.00	2.81
1974	2,680,800	2.70[a]	3.49

SOURCE: Honduras, interpolations based on estimates compiled from Johannessen 1963 and on data from HDGEC 1932, 1952, 1964a, 1977; El Salvador, see Table 2.1.

[a] Reflects loss of Salvadorean immigrants.

suggest. As in El Salvador, the population is largely rural and dependent on agriculture. Considering both the density differential and the relative size of farms, one might reasonably expect Hondurans to have higher average incomes than their Salvadorean neighbors. But that is not the case. As F. T. Bachmura notes, this situation runs counter to the trend in other parts of Latin America, where "migration is characteristically from countries of low average income to countries of higher average income. Migration flows from Colombia to Venezuela, from Guatemala to Mexico, and from Mexico to the United States. In the case of El Salvador and Honduras, however, the situation is reversed. People migrate from a country with a higher per-capita income to a country with a lower per-capita income" (1971: 285). The annual per-capita income in Honduras in 1950 was only U.S. $138, compared with $201 in El Salvador (ECLA 1961; CONAPLAN, *Indicadores* 1964). Thus, far from moving to a land of abundance and opportunity, Salvadorean migrants entered a country where people were on the whole economically worse off than back at home.

This paradoxical situation suggests that it may be seriously misleading to compare the two countries on the basis of their total population and resource statistics. We know, for a start, from our discussion of El Salvador, that figures on the average availability of land or cash income can conceal a substantial amount of variability within a population. As discussed in Chapter One, the distribution of resources may then cause average estimates to give a false impression of abundance. Beyond this, simple density gradient arguments sometimes carry an implicit assumption that the relevant resources are at least roughly proportional to the total land area in a given region. But if the resource in question is not simple personal space or *lebensraum*, this assumption, too, may be seriously in error.

In fact, in the case of El Salvador and Honduras, comparisons of aggregate data introduce errors of both kinds. Consider first the question of resources and surface area. Here a comparison of total land area is particularly misleading because of the important physiographic differences between the two countries. For one thing, Honduras is far more mountainous than El Salvador. One study, for example, estimates that 60.8 percent of its surface area slopes at more than 40 percent, rendering this land useless for everything but grazing and forestry (OAS 1963). Moreover, unlike El Salvador, Honduras has little fertile soil, since "the volcanic axis of Central America skirts [its] southern edge . . . , leaving but a few volcanos as islets within the Gulf of Fonseca. Honduras thus lacks the coverage of recent volcanic ash that has created the fertile soils of Central America's Pacific versant" (West & Augelli 1976: 427). Owing to this combination of geographical features, even the most optimistic of three recent studies of the country's soil-use potential estimates that only 32.4 percent of the land is suitable for any kind of agriculture (see Table 4.3).*

Actual land-use patterns in Honduras reflect these limitations. As indicated in Table 4.1, Honduras's more than five-to-one size advantage over El Salvador shrinks to a 1.53 : 1 ratio when the comparison is based on land in farms, and to a negligible 1.11 : 1 ratio when only cropland is considered. In other words, though Honduras has over 433 percent more total land than El Salvador, it has only 11 percent more land under cultivation.

The choice of denominator or land base for density comparisons can therefore have a major influence on the conclusions reached. The

* In contrast, the agricultural land-use potential of El Salvador has been estimated at 64.4 percent of the total, or 1,355,900 hectares out of a total of 2,104,100 (ESMAG 1977: 147).

same is true for the population defined as the numerator. To compare the availability of agricultural resources on the basis of total population size can be seriously misleading. Looking at Tables 2.2 and 4.4, for example, we see that in 1961 nearly 80 percent of Honduras's population was rural, compared with only 70 percent for El Salvador, and that 67 percent of its economically active population was in agriculture, compared with El Salvador's 60 percent.

These considerations combine to give an altogether different impression of ecological conditions in Honduras from those implied by total density comparisons. As shown in Table 4.5 and Figure 4.3, the

T A B L E 4.3   *The Land-Use Potential of Honduras*

		Area suitable for agriculture	
Source	Area covered in study (hectares)	Hectares	Percent of total area studied
OAS 1963	9,463,450[a]	2,304,750	24.4%
Plath 1967	11,172,790[b]	1,992,770	17.8
Consuplan 1974	11,208,800	3,634,180	32.4

[a] Excludes all territory east of the 85th meridian, i.e., roughly the portion excluded from Fig. 4.1.
[b] Thought to be the total national land area at the time. The total area is now calculated to be 11,208,800.

T A B L E 4.4   *Characteristics of the Population of Honduras, 1887–1974*

		Rural population[a]		Economically active population[b]	
Year	Censused population	Percent of total population	Percent agriculturally active	Percent of total population	Percent agriculturally active
1887	331,917	95.01%	27.43%[c]	29.75 %[c]	87.60%[d]
1930	854,184	87.92	27.43	29.75	81.07
1950	1,368,605	84.50	25.35	29.35	72.99
1961	1,884,765	79.69	25.24	30.14	66.75
1974	2,656,948	69.78	24.84	28.71	60.38

SOURCE: Vallejo 1888; HDGEC 1932, 1952, 1954, 1964a, 1964b, 1977.
[a] Recalculated for each year from census information using 2,500 or more inhabitants as the criterion for urban.
[b] Recalculated for 1930 and 1950 from census information on occupational status in order to be consistent with later definitions.
[c] 1930 figures used as conservative estimate for 1887 percentages.
[d] Estimate derived from other assumptions for 1887.

TABLE 4.5 *Four Measures of the Population Density of El Salvador and Honduras in the 1960's*

(*People per square kilometer*)

Category	El Salvador	Honduras	Ratio El Salvador to Honduras
Total density	119.92	16.82	7.13
Rural density[a]	84.30	13.40	6.29
Agricultural density[b]	30.75	15.67	1.96
Arable density[c]	101.43	71.18	1.43

SOURCE: ESDGEC 1965, 1967; HDGEC 1964a, 1968.

NOTE: The density calculations are based on 1961 population data for both countries.

[a] 1961 rural population (by the 2,500+ inhabitants urban criterion) divided by total land area.

[b] 1961 agriculturally active population divided by land in farms. The figures on farmland and cropland for Honduras are for 1965–66.

[c] 1961 agriculturally active population divided by land in cultivation.

density differential between El Salvador and Honduras diminishes from 7.13 for total density to 1.43 when the measures used are the people actually engaged in agriculture and the land actually under cultivation. By these measures, there is only 43 percent more arable land per cultivator in Honduras, not 613 percent. The only inference one can draw from a more detailed density analysis, therefore, is that land is somewhat less scarce in Honduras than in El Salvador. The difference does not suggest great overabundance among the famous "fragrant pines" of Honduras.

But even this recalculated per-capita land advantage is misleading when soil fertility is also taken into account. Let us again take maize production as an indicator. Honduras had an average maize yield of 756.6 kilograms per hectare in 1952, compared with El Salvador's average of 1,148.6 in 1950 (HDGEC 1954; ESDGEC 1954). If we compute an average production differential for 1950–52, reducing Honduras's 43 percent size advantage by a 65.9 percent yield disadvantage, our indicator suggests that total productivity in Honduras is only 94.2 percent of that in El Salvador. Such a difference has persisted since the 1950's, despite improved yields in both countries. Thus, though Honduras's average maize yield rose to 1,081.3 kilograms per hectare in 1974, this was still only 62.3 percent of El Salvador's 1971 average of 1,736.9 (HDGEC 1975; ESDGEC 1975).

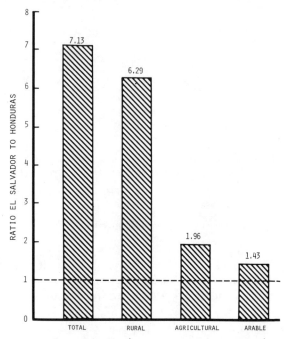

Fig. 4.3. Four measures of the population density of El Salvador and Honduras in the 1960's. Rural density: rural population divided by total land area. Agricultural density: agriculturally active population divided by land in farms. Arable density: agriculturally active population divided by land in cultivation. SOURCE: See Table 4.5.

Statistically speaking, Honduras's cropland advantage is virtually eliminated because of its poor soil. In terms of aggregate statistics, at least, Honduras hardly looks like a comparative "land of plenty" next to El Salvador.

The Distribution of Farmland

Relying on aggregate data to compare access to land can also be misleading. As we saw earlier, the use of average figures for land availability in El Salvador greatly underestimates resource scarcity in that country. In 1961, for example, 85.2 percent of the farms were smaller than the average farm size of 6.97 hectares; and by 1971,

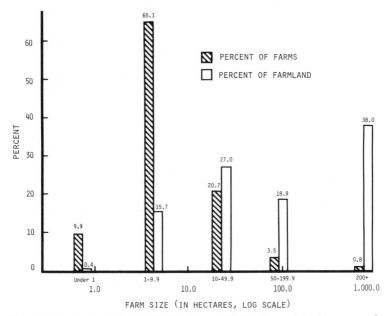

Fig. 4.4. Distribution of farmland in Honduras, 1952. The figure shows histograms of the percentages of the total number and area of farms in the same size classes as used for El Salvador (see Fig. 2.12). SOURCE: HDGEC 1954.

though the average size had dropped by more than a hectare, to 5.36 hectares, the proportion of below-average farms had risen to 86.7 percent. In addition, in 1971 80.5 percent of the agriculturally active population worked plots smaller than the per-capita average of 2.5 hectares (Table 2.3).

The Honduran agricultural census figures reveal much the same pattern of unequal distribution.* Figure 4.4 shows the distribution of farmland in Honduras in 1952, drawn on the same scale as Figure 2.12 for El Salvador. Although the farms in Honduras are generally larger

* Unfortunately, only the 1952 census allows direct size class comparisons with the data from El Salvador. The complete 1974 census was not available at the time of writing, and the preceding one is lacking in important respects. Unlike the 1952 census, for example, the 1965–66 census is compiled in manzanas, so that equivalent size classes cannot be constructed. Worse still, for this study, all sizes below five manzanas are rounded to an integer value. In addition, no production figures are given by size of farm, precluding the analogue of Figure 2.16 for that agricultural year.

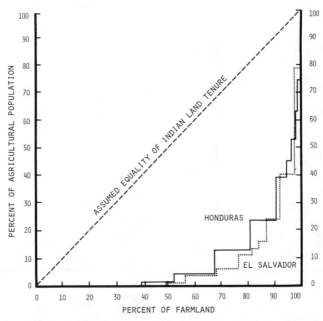

Fig. 4.5. Comparison of land concentration in El Salvador (in 1971) and Honduras (in 1965–66). The histogram for Honduras allows for 113,616 landless workers in 1965–66 (26.1 percent of the agricultural population). SOURCE: Honduras, HDGEC 1967; CEPAL 1970: 70. El Salvador, same as Fig. 2.14 (Phase III).

than in El Salvador, their relative distribution into size classes is similarly skewed. In 1952, a full 75.0 percent of the Honduran farms were under ten hectares but accounted for only 16.1 percent of the total land in farms. At the other extreme, 38 percent of the farmland was held by the 0.8 percent of farms in the over-200-hectare class. These figures are comparable with their 1961 Salvadorean counterparts, i.e., under ten hectares, 91.4 percent of the farms, with 21.9 percent of the farmland; over 200 hectares, 0.5 percent of the farms, with 37.7 percent of the land. Further, the largest farms in Honduras, those with more than 500 hectares, held 709,304 hectares (28.2 percent of the total farmland), or roughly 1.76 times as much as all the 117,103 farms in the under-ten-hectare class. As a result of this concentration, about 82 percent of all Honduran farms in 1952 fell below the average size of 16.06 hectares.

Figure 4.5 gives a closer comparison of land concentration in El

Salvador and Honduras. Plotting the percent of the agricultural population against the percent of the land they use has the advantage of ignoring the relative sizes of farms. This enables a direct comparison of the 1965–66 data for Honduras and the 1971 data for El Salvador. The plot was prepared using the same assumptions as for Figure 2.14 (Phase III) above. The curve allows for 113,616 landless Honduran agriculturalists in 1965–66 (26.1 percent of the total agricultural population), as estimated by CEPAL 1970: 70 (see also CEPAL 1973).

Several features of this figure are worth noting. First, it shows slightly less concentration of farmland in Honduras than in El Salvador in the largest farm-size categories (38.5 percent, compared with 49.3 percent). Second, this difference continues through the mid-range categories. Until the 90 percent of farmland point is reached, the Honduran data show a higher percent-of-population value. Third, small farmers and landless workers actually have access to a smaller proportion of the total farmland in Honduras than in El Salvador. As shown in the figure, the distribution curve for Honduras crosses to the right of the Salvadorean curve for the last three size classes (i.e., all farms under 3.0 manzanas, or 2.1 hectares). Part of this reversal is due to the greater percentage of landless agriculturalists in Honduras (26.1 compared with 21.8), even using the 1971 figure for El Salvador. The CEPAL figure I have used here to ensure a comparable estimate with El Salvador is, however, based on sound methodology and is well in line with both previous and more recent estimates (HDGEC 1954; IIES 1961: 93; INA 1976). A large part of the difference in landless populations stems from the sizable proportion of the agriculturally active population employed as wage labor on the banana plantations in Honduras (about 16,000 people in 1965).

This diagram, then, has an important implication for the study of the ecological origins of conflict between El Salvador and Honduras. Although Honduras has more land and larger farms than El Salvador, the pattern of land distribution has made the land-shortage problem of the small farmers there no less acute there than it is across the border.

Historical Trends of Land Distribution

Phase I: The colonial and early republican periods. Although comparatively little is known about the history of land tenure changes in Honduras, the available evidence indicates that the degree of concentration discussed above is the product of a historically accelerating

114   *The Question of Resource Abundance in Honduras*

T A B L E 4.6   *Land Titles Issued in Honduras, 1600–1949*

	Total grants		Ejidal		Private property	
Period	Number	Percent of grand total	Number	Percent of period total	Number	Percent of period total
1600–1649	47	1.5%	5	10.6%	42	89.4%
1650–1699	155	4.7	9	5.8	144	92.9
1700–1749	417	12.7	43	10.3	360	86.3
1750–1799	269	8.2	39	14.5	212	78.8
1800–1849	519	15.8	129	24.9	377	72.6
1850–1899	1,265	38.5	213	16.8	1,020	80.6
1900–1949	615	18.6	99	16.1	496	80.7
TOTAL	3,287[a]	100.0	537	—	2,651	—

SOURCE: Pérez Brignoli 1973a: 66.

[a] Not shown but included in this total are 99 titles given as "collective property" to convents and Indian villages.

process. As in El Salvador, the major distributional inequalities began with the Spanish conquest (see Villanueva 1968a; Fonck 1972; Peréz Brignoli 1973a, 1973b). In contrast to El Salvador, however, livestock production was the predominant agricultural enterprise from the earliest colonial years.

The small privileged minority of colonial times in Honduras came to see in private ownership of large tracts of land ... the basis of their own survival. Livestock production came to be a highly profitable enterprise in the large landholding units. . . . From the beginning of the colonial period, private ownership of land was given to knights, captains, and squires of the imperial states in amounts measured by *caballerías* (loosely translated as knight's units) while private property in land was given to the Spanish soldiers and peons—in the lower echelons of colonial society—in amounts measured by *peonías* (i.e., peon's units), with the former units being hundreds of times larger than the latter ones (Villanueva 1968b, cited in K. H. Parsons 1976: 2).

A compilation of the land titles of the period (see Table 4.6) shows that 49 land grants were registered between 1600 and 1649, during what Murdo MacLeod (1973) terms "the first great era of land grants" in Central America. More than 85 percent of these grants were private concessions, as shown in the table, including one of the largest grants in all of Central America in the early seventeenth century—a tract of 16 caballerías (721 hectares) that was given to a monastic order near

Choluteca in 1607 (MacLeod 1973: 302). Six of the other grants in the southern region in that period were large enough to accommodate 30,000 cattle among them (*ibid.*, p. 304).

Thereafter, the number of private grants proliferated and continued to constitute the bulk of the recognized land claims, as shown in the table. In this case, however, the rapid conversion of territory to private plots did not result in the abolition of communal and ejidal lands, as in El Salvador. On the contrary, after independence the country's land laws (in 1836, 1870, and 1936) deliberately encouraged ejidal grants to communities in order to protect and guarantee the small farmer's access to land (Stokes 1947; IIES 1961b; K. T. Parsons 1976). That policy is reflected in the increased share of ejidal grants beginning in the period 1800–1849 (Table 4.6). According to Charles A. Brand (1972), even by the 1880's and 1890's there was still little competition between communal claims to the land, concentrated in the western mountainous areas, and the growing demand for private property. Because of a poorly developed transportation system and a lack of capital among the country's elite, Honduras did not share in the Central American coffee boom of 1880–1930 (Brand 1972; Peréz Brignoli 1973b). The preservation, indeed the growth, of communal forms of land tenure meant that as late as the 1880's "each department had sufficient agricultural land and each *campesino* was able to have the land necessary to support himself and his family" (Carías & Slutzky 1971: 34; see also IIES 1961b: 23).

Phase II: The impact of banana cultivation. The next major change in land tenure in Honduras occurred with the explosive growth of commercial banana production in the Caribbean coastal lowlands. Figure 4.6 shows the exponential rise in the country's banana exports between 1900 and 1930 (measured by their value) and the ensuing crash of the industry under the combined forces of the world depression and the spread of leafspot disease (*Cercospora musae*). The pattern is strongly reminiscent of the cotton boom and bust in El Salvador. The figure also shows the value of total exports from Honduras, including returns from cattle sold abroad and mineral ores from the few surviving mines. A comparison of the two curves clearly shows the country's heavy dependence on the banana trade for the generation of foreign exchange, particularly in the pre-1930 period.

The banana boom saw both an expansion of agriculture into vast

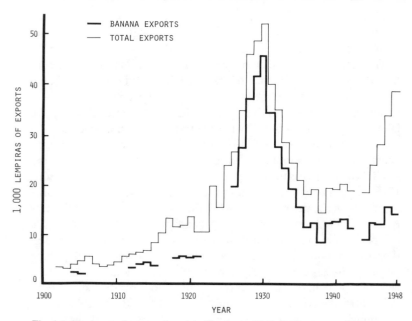

Fig. 4.6. The banana boom and crash in Honduras, 1902–1948. SOURCE: Márquez et al. 1950; ECLA 1961: 25; Laínez & Meza 1973; Meza & López 1973.

new areas and a consolidation of the control of those lands. Until 1899, bananas were sold by small independent producers to 22 separate marketing companies (Laínez & Meza 1973). But United States holding companies and fruit dealers moved into the market at that point, attracted by the government's offer of large tracts of land suitable for banana cultivation in return for the construction of railroads. These companies soon out-competed the small producers and shippers. By 1910, 80 percent of all the banana lands were under the control of United States firms (Brand 1972: 159). In 1914, the five principal concessionaires held a total of 416,500 hectares of coastal land, much of it the most fertile land in Honduras (Laínez & Meza 1973: 139). The consolidation process continued until 1929, when the United Fruit Company bought out its last major competitor, the Cuyamel Fruit Company, and thereby gained a virtual monopoly of the country's banana production.

In terms of the land resources of the country, then, the trend toward concentration that began gradually under Spanish rule was greatly intensified with the establishment of banana export agriculture. Additional large areas of farmland were given over to the control of a few big private producers. Because this land was sparsely inhabited in the early 1900's and located far from the areas of traditional cultivation, the process did not greatly affect the supply of land to small farmers at the time.

Sixty years later, however, when malaria and the other tropical diseases that had discouraged campesino settlement in the Caribbean lowland areas had been brought under control, the land that was still in the hands of foreign banana companies (200,000 hectares, according to Carías & Slutzky 1971: 41) was plainly needed by, but inaccessible to, a rural population that had quadrupled since 1900. This land, together with the area in large estates in other regions of Honduras, meant that peasant cultivators were competitively excluded from 38 percent of the total farmland in 1961. This exclusion, in turn, meant that most of the rural population growth had to be absorbed in the western and southern departments—areas already densely populated. What began as an attempt to "develop" untapped national resources on the north coast therefore came to have the ironic consequence of intensifying land scarcity and poverty in other areas.

Phase III: The growth of commercial agriculture. The final phase of land concentration in Honduras began with the expansion and diversification of commercial agriculture after World War II. Unlike the banana growth phase, which affected land tenure in a sparsely populated region, this phase, involving growth in the coffee, cotton, and cattle industries, affected areas of traditional agriculture and relatively dense settlement. As Kenneth H. Parsons notes (1976: 9): "Since World War II, events have gradually closed in on the campesinos. Land for subsistence crops [has become] increasingly hard to get, due partly to the increase in numbers of rural people, and partly to changes in the structure of opportunities for the use of land, which make large-scale farming more profitable." Among the postwar changes, improved internal road networks and new links with outside markets (including the Pan-American Highway) were particularly instrumental in stimulating the large-scale production of cotton and cattle.

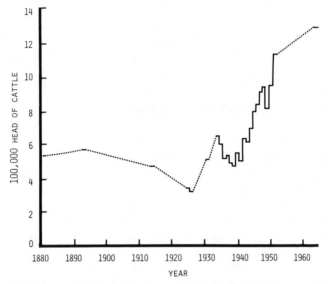

Fig. 4.7. Cattle production in Honduras, 1881–1966. Dotted lines connect non-sequential estimates and census totals. SOURCE: Estimates, Johannessen 1963: 46. Census counts, HDGEC 1954, 1968.

Some idea of the magnitude and effect of these increases in commercial agriculture can be gleaned from Figure 4.7, which charts the growth of the cattle industry between 1881 and 1965. As we see, that industry stagnated or declined during the years of the banana industry's most explosive growth. And it continued to make little or no headway in the early 1940's. But then, following World War II, cattle production began to increase dramatically, with the total count doubling between 1939 and 1950. The increase continued through the 1950's, adding another 14 percent between the agricultural censuses of 1952 and 1965–66.*

Most of this increase, as we can see in Figure 4.8, took place on large farms. In 1952, for example, farms of less than 50 hectares raised 74.0

---

* According to James Parsons (1976: 125), Honduran production of beef doubled again between the early 1960's and 1972. With these increases in the cattle herd came an expansion of the country's pastureland, which grew from 823,000 hectares in 1952 to 1,131,000 in 1966 (HDGEC 1954, 1968). This rapid expansion of cattle and pasture in Honduras is part of what Parsons terms Central America's "Grassland Revolution"

percent of the country's cattle; by 1966 such farms produced only 45.3 percent of the expanded total head of cattle. (In this connection, see Murga Frassinetti 1973).

Cotton and coffee production also sharply increased in the postwar years. The area planted to coffee doubled in 15 years, rising from 45,000 hectares in 1945 to more than 90,000 hectares in 1959, and production rose from 10,000 metric tons to 24,000. In the same period the area planted in cotton grew from less than 400 hectares to 9,000 hectares, and production rose from 100 metric tons to 4,000.

Although the 1965–66 agricultural census does not provide the statistics to determine the farm sizes involved in these increases, there is some evidence, particularly for cotton, that here too much of the expansion took place on larger-than-average farms. Consider first Figure 4.9, the analogue of Figure 2.17 for El Salvador. The figure shows the cumulative production totals for the most important food crop in Honduras, maize, and the most important export crop, bananas, as a function of farm size. The data are from the 1952 census year, which conveniently corresponds to the midpoint of the 1945–59 growth interval we have been discussing. Like the corresponding El Salvador figure, the graph includes cumulative percent plots of the total farmland and the total number of farms. These curves together indicate that the production of food crops is even more concentrated on small farms in Honduras than in El Salvador. The incremental production of maize very closely parallels the curve for the number of farms, rather than the farmland curve. As indicated by the dotted line, in 1952 farms of less than five hectares (57 percent of the total number) grew nearly 40 percent of the nation's maize on only 8.1 percent of the farmland.* A later study (OAS 1963) found a similar concentration in the production of the country's other basic foodcrops, rice and beans. In contrast, the banana production curve is similar to the coffee curve in El Salvador, with large farms producing disproportionate amounts of the export crop in both cases.

---

since World War II. Responding largely to economic opportunities outside the national market, exports of beef have grown to account for more than one-half of the annual production (this is also true in Costa Rica and Nicaragua, though not in El Salvador; see J. Parsons 1976: 125). Ironically, as Parsons notes, the average per-capita domestic consumption has actually decreased in the same period.

* In El Salvador, it will be recalled, the farms in this size class (85.2 percent of the total) grew 58 percent of the country's maize on 15.6 percent of the farmland.

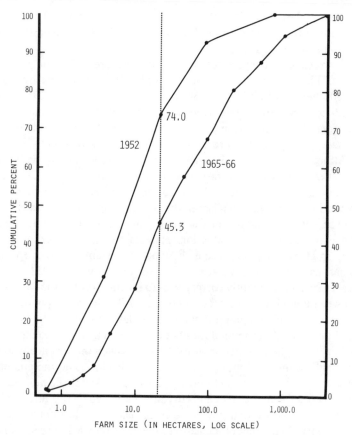

Fig. 4.8. Cattle production by farm size in Honduras, 1952 and 1965–66. SOURCE: HDGEC 1954, 1967.

In the midst of the rapid expansion of new forms of commercial agriculture, then, the production of food crops in Honduras remained concentrated on small farms. Only a very small fraction came from the farms of 100 hectares or more. However, between 1952 and 1966 the amount of land dedicated to annual crops on these farms suddenly increased by 56.3 percent, compared with a 15.2 percent increase for farms of all sizes (HDGEC 1954, 1967). It is very likely that most of the 12,700 hectares involved were used for cotton. Unpublished cen-

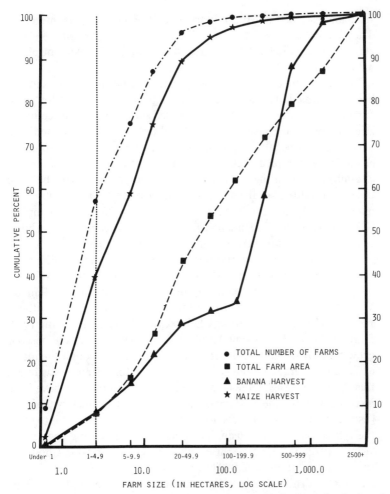

Fig. 4.9. Crop production by farm size in Honduras, 1952. As shown by the dotted vertical line, farms of less than 5.0 hectares produce 39.5 percent of the maize on 8.1 percent of the farmland. SOURCE: HDGEC 1954.

sus data described in Murga Frassinetti 1973 support this inference. They show that in 1965 a mere 272 landholdings in the 350+ -hectare class accounted for 5,750 hectares of cotton, or 36.8 percent of the national total.

This expansion of commercial production on large landholdings had two immediate effects on the availability of farmland for small farmers. First, the value of land increased sharply across the country, affecting both purchase price and rental fees. For the estimated 16.6 percent of all agricultural families that depended on rented lands, for example, rents typically changed from payments in kind (e.g., sacks of grain) to cash in the years of higher cotton prices, and at the same time their value rose from approximately three to five *lempiras* per manzana (1 lempira = U.S. $.50) to between 20 and 30 lempiras (CEPAL 1970; K. H. Parsons 1976: 15). But the campesino's ability to pay such amounts increased only marginally in that period.

Second, and more important, the expansion of commercial agriculture created a competitive threat to land in other forms of non-property tenure (ejidal, national, and untitled, or *ocupante*, lands). Various studies of land tenure and peasant economy in the southern region of Honduras, including Choluteca and Valle (R. A. White 1972; Stares 1972; K. H. Parsons 1976), indicate that much of the postwar growth in cattle and cotton production took place through the illegal expansion of large haciendas. Rodney Stares, for instance, has found that "in many cases, large areas of ejidal and national land have been incorporated by the systematic extension of hacienda boundaries [usually for the price of barbed-wire fencing], usurping in this manner the rights of ejidal-land using peasants with titles dating back many years" (1972: 38). He cites the example of two haciendas in Choluteca that alone added some 22,000 hectares to their holdings between 1952 and 1966 in this fashion. The expansion of the Hacienda San Bernardo in Choluteca is illustrative of this process:

For years the small farmers of Azacualpas had been moving into the area bordering the Hacienda San Bernardo to make their milpas, and they gradually were establishing permanent homes there. They had always considered the land to be national and open for occupation. In the early 1950's, at the beginning of the cotton and cattle boom, the owner of the hacienda fenced in the whole area, had the settlers removed by force, and jailed any who resisted the removal. . . .

In 1954, by order of the Ministry of Government, some fifty families were evicted from their plots. It was a case of public office acting in collusion with the powerful against the small farmer. The land was largely utilized in cotton production rather than in basic grains. The owner did not personally manage the hacienda but rented out more than 700 manzanas of land at the price of $40 per manzana. Much of the land was used extensively in the pasture of cattle. (Later, when the land was expropriated, it was discovered that most of it was national land.)

In the mid-1950's the whole neighborhood was fenced in with barbed wire, and the farmers had to crawl through fences to get to water or to the school. They were forbidden to collect kindling in the area, and various men were accused of stealing wood and were jailed by order of the owner. The plantings of bananas and the fruit trees that some of the families had put in were destroyed. (R. A. White, quoted in Capa & Stycos 1974: 128)

This process was repeated in "community after community" in the 1950's and 1960's, according to Kenneth Parsons (1976:16), becoming known as the Enclosure Movement.

Further examples of this kind of encroachment and of the Honduran campesino's response will be described in the next two chapters. The point to be made here is simply that the expansion of commercial agriculture on large holdings was responsible for a considerable reduction of non-property land in the 1950's and 1960's. This reduction not only directly affected the supply of land for small farmers in many of the country's most densely settled areas, but also took place in the face of rapid rural population growth. These changes had synergistic effects, greatly accelerating the process of land concentration.

Salvadorean Immigration and the Land Shortage in Honduras

It was precisely at this time, when land was becoming scarcer and scarcer for the small farmer, that the stream of migrants from El Salvador reached its greatest volume. The timing and magnitude of this migration clearly had the potential to contribute in an important way to the land scarcity problem in Honduras. The estimated 300,000 Salvadoreans living in Honduras in 1969 represented more than 12 percent of the country's total population, or roughly one person in eight. As many as half of these people, as we saw in Chapter Two, arrived after the beginning of the boom in commercial agriculture. That fact is especially significant, in terms of the land shortage in

Honduras, for it suggests that the migration was largely of a rural-to-rural type. Indeed, there is other evidence to support this point.*

There is no question, for example, that the banana boom on the north coast attracted a good number of migrant laborers from El Salvador. Indeed, according to Capa and Stycos (1974: 44), that migration was actually encouraged by the banana export companies in Honduras, which considered Salvadoreans highly desirable workers. This was corroborated by one of my informants in Tenancingo, who told me that he had been recruited to work on a banana farm in the 1920's by agents of the United Fruit Company headquartered in San Salvador. In the mid-1960's, according to one estimate, 30 percent of all the workers on the Honduran banana plantations were Salvadoreans, or about 4,800 in a total labor force of 16,000 (Torres-Rivas 1971: 206). Considering that there were substantial layoffs in the 1950's, and that the companies were under increasing pressure to hire Hondurans, there were probably many more Salvadoreans at work on the plantations in earlier years. A good number of Salvadoreans were among the 19,000 landless workers who were released by the companies in the 1950's and forced to seek land or employment elsewhere (Posas Amador 1976). Many of these people remained in rural areas and began to work farms for themselves (Carías & Slutzky 1971: 31).

We also know that the majority of the Soccer War refugees had lived in the countryside and worked in agriculture. In the de Paredes study (1969), for example, 110 of the 140 family heads in the sample (78.7 percent) had worked in some agricultural capacity; and 90 of the 110 (81.8 percent) had worked land for themselves, either as renters (51), owners (33), or squatters on national land (6). Significantly, two-thirds of the owners had owned five manzanas or more: 15 had owned five to 25 manzanas, five had owned 25 to 50 manzanas, and two had owned more than 100 manzanas.

A similar picture emerges from the responses of the refugees interviewed by Capa and Stycos (1974). Almost without exception, the

* Certainly, that was the traditional pattern. As early as 1890, the Honduran census showed that "the great majority of non-Hondurans were the almost 5,000 Guatemalans and Salvadoreans, mostly subsistence-type farmers settled along the Western frontiers" (Brand 1972: 57). More specific data in the 1895 census indicates that 75.4 percent of the 6,021 foreigners in the country resided in Choluteca, Valle, La Paz, Copán, Gracias, and Intibuca. These departments, located along or near the Salvadorean border, represented the very backbone of traditional agriculture in Honduras.

men claimed that they had farmed under better conditions in Honduras than in El Salvador. The informant-refugee I mentioned earlier, who had returned, in 1969, with a group of 200 natives of the Quezalapa valley (i.e., Tenancingo and the adjacent municipality of Cinquera), concurred. The son of landless peasants, he had moved with his parents to Honduras in 1917 at the age of eight, to settle in a mountainous area near the border. By the time he was thirty, the family owned ten manzanas, including a small orchard. This was all lost with the war.

Finally, we have estimates from both governments that point to the overwhelmingly rural composition of the migrants. El Salvador's National Planning Office estimated that 28.2 percent of the refugees had been economically active in the agricultural sector, and that these people represented 76.9 percent of the economically active refugee population (CONAPLAN 1969)—a figure that closely matches the de Paredes estimate of 78.7 percent. Applying the 28.2 percent figure to the estimated 300,000 Salvadoreans in Honduras in 1969 puts the number of agriculturalists at 84,600. This would mean that Salvadoreans constituted 19.8 percent of the estimated 427,000 agriculturally active persons in Honduras in 1969—or about one person in five.

From Honduras we have a second set of estimates for 1969, made by Rigoberto Sandoval Corea, then director of the National Agrarian Institute. Since this institute was charged with carrying out an agrarian reform law passed in 1962 that excluded all but Honduran citizens by birth from agrarian reform projects, it had gathered considerable information on the use of Honduran territory by Salvadoreans. According to Sandoval Corea, "At the time of the outbreak of hostilities there were 219,619 Salvadoreans without legal papers in Honduras, representing approximately 36,000 campesino families, and occupying an area of 293,000 manzanas of national land" (*El Cronista,* Tegucigalpa, July 11, 1969, quoted in Carías & Slutzky 1971: 294). By these figures, Salvadoreans accounted for 14.9 percent of the rural families in Honduras and occupied about 8.5 percent of the total area in farms. They suggest that the Salvadorean families in Honduras had access to an average of 8.1 manzanas (5.7 hectares). This figure is well above the land area available to the majority of rural families in El Salvador and to the poorer half of the rural families of Honduras. Furthermore, these figures indicate that the Salvadorean migrants had among them almost twice as much land as the total for all the farms in Honduras in 1966 of less than five manzanas. Remembering that these farms account for 47.2 percent of the country's total, it seems reasonable to infer that the Salvadorean migration had a major competitive effect in reducing the land supply available to small farmers in Honduras. This inference is examined more closely in the next chapter.

To conclude, it is clear that land has rapidly grown more scarce for small farmers in Honduras since the close of World War II. Three developments have contributed to this trend, namely, the expansion of commercial agriculture, which increased the value of land and reduced the amount of non-property acreage; a gradual but accelerating "filling up" of the rural communities with the descendants of the original inhabitants (R. A. White 1972: 37); and the presence of as many as 300,000 Salvadoreans, of whom 80,000 or more worked directly in agriculture, primarily as small-scale cultivators (see also A. White 1973: 185).

Consistent with this picture of "events closing in" on the Honduran campesinos is the country's remarkable rate of urban growth after World War II, due largely to rural out-migration. The city of San Pedro Sula, for example, had a net population increase of nearly 500 percent between 1950 and 1970 (Teller 1972: 31). Though many of the migrants who contributed to this increase had resided briefly in other towns before arriving in San Pedro Sula, the majority were born in rural communities (again using the 2,500 criterion). Nearly half of these were from the poor and crowded departments along the western border. Similarly, the capital city of Tegucigalpa has been growing by more than 6 percent a year since about 1950. More than half of that growth has been ascribed to in-migration rather than natural increase. And again, most of the new arrivals were found to have come from rural areas in a step-wise migration process (Brunn & Thomas 1972, 1973).

In the next chapter we will study one of the rural communities that has been both a source of this urban in-migration and a destination for the immigrants from El Salvador.

CHAPTER FIVE

Scarcity, Survival, and Salvadoreans in Langue

As discussed in Chapter Four, the small farmers of Honduras faced a rapidly growing scarcity of land after World War II. At the same time, increasing numbers of El Salvador's landless and land-poor peasants came to live in Honduras, further increasing the demand for arable land. It is reasonable, therefore, to hypothesize that Salvadorean immigrants contributed significantly to the process of land competition in Honduras. It is also reasonable to hypothesize that the Honduran small farmers would have been the most affected. For one thing, it is clear that most of the migrants were far too poor to purchase or even rent a medium to large farm. The majority, by all accounts, became renters, sharecroppers, or *ocupantes* (squatters), the very groups that were most hard pressed for land in the Honduran society. In addition, we could reasonably expect the livelihood of small farmers to be more sensitive to competitive losses. As we saw in Chapter Three, even a relatively small incremental loss from the land base of a poor peasant family may have serious consequences for its ability to survive and reproduce. The same loss to the owner of a large estate could have little or no effect.

Table 5.1 illustrates one of the reasons why poor peasants were unable to absorb such losses. As we see, Honduran farmers with less than 10.0 hectares in 1952 tended to have more than 56 percent of their land under cultivation, compared with a mere 7 percent for the farmers with 50.0 hectares or more. This pattern of land use by farm size is similar to that noted for El Salvador (Fig. 2.16), but here it has additional significance. Because the soils in most areas of the country are poor, Honduran farmland generally requires two to three years of fallow for every year of use to maintain even a minimum standard of fertility. As the table indicates, however, the small farmers can ill-

T A B L E 5.1   *Land Use by Farm Size in Honduras, 1952*

Farm size in hectares	Hectares of farmland	Total land in cultivation		Implied fallow-to-cultivation ratio per year[a]
		Hectares	Percent of total farmland	
<1.0	9,991	8,673	86.8%	0.15
1.0–9.9	393,795	221,221	56.2	0.78
10.0–49.9	676,495	148,760	22.0	3.55
50.0–199.9	451,855	30,596	6.8	13.77
200.0 and over	953,468	49,020	5.1	18.45

SOURCE: HDGEC 1954.

[a] The number of years a hectare of land can be left fallow for each year it is planted in crops with this land-use pattern. Calculated for each farm size as 1 divided by the percent in crops minus 1.

afford to take their land out of cultivation. Even those with as much as 9.0 hectares are essentially forced to till their land at least every other year. Land use of this intensity invariably causes diminishing harvests as time goes by. Therefore, even without the competition of Salvadorean immigrants, the overworking of the land can mean the eroding of the family livelihood. Under these circumstances, any additional decrease in access to land brought about by outside competitors could have greatly exaggerated consequences.

In order to determine what impact the Salvadoreans had on land availability in Honduras, I conducted a local-level study in a second municipality called Langue. This study, though much like my Tenancingo investigation in many respects, was designed to provide answers to four specific questions: (1) Is it true that Honduran peasants are faced with disproportionately small and declining yields from their plots? (2) Are they therefore confronted with land-related survival exigencies similar to those in El Salvador? (3) Is there any evidence that the Salvadorean immigrants exacerbated the situation and further reduced the lands available to the Honduran peasants? (4) If so, can we then link the land competition among small farmers to the expulsion of the Salvadoreans from the country in 1969? The results of the study are summarized in this chapter.

Physical and Historical Features of Langue

Like Tenancingo, Langue was selected as a study site on the basis of its conformity to characteristics of small-farmer agriculture in Hon-

T A B L E 5.2   *Selection Criteria for the Honduras Study Site*

	1965–66 census figures	
Criteria	National average	Langue
Average farm size (hectares)	13.56	5.10
Distribution of farms by size class (percent)		
<1.0 hectare	15.0%	22.9%
1.0–3.4 hectares	32.2	30.3
3.5–6.9 hectares	20.4	22.6
7.0–13.9 hectares	15.2	16.9
14.0–34.9 hectares	11.2	6.3
35.0 hectares and over	6.0	1.0
Owner-operated farms (percent)	25.4%	49.6%
Land use (percent)		
Perennial crops	7.9%	1.5%
Annual crops, including fallow land[a]	23.4	46.9
Pasture	46.7	24.9
Woodland and scrub	19.0	19.3
Other	3.0	7.4
Average yields (kilograms/hectare)		
Maize	1,033	546
Sorghum	742	705
Beans	605	581

SOURCE: HDGEC 1968.

[a] Data are not available for annual export and non-export crops as shown in Table 3.1. However, in 1965–66, 46.4 percent of all the annual cropland in Langue was planted in the most important non-export crop, maize, compared with the national average of 40.6 percent.

duras (see Table 5.2). It should be noted that at 5.10 hectares, the average farm in this community is actually closer to the average size farm in El Salvador (5.36 hectares) than to the national average, and is nearly twice as large as the average farm plot in Tenancingo (2.82 hectares; see Table 3.1). This size advantage, however, is virtually eliminated by lower yields. The average maize yield in Langue, for example, is 546 kilograms per hectare, compared with Tenancingo's 1,183 kilograms per hectare (for non-hybrid varieties).

The municipality of Langue is situated in the south of Honduras in the department of Valle, approximately 20 kilometers inland from the Gulf of Fonseca and 15 kilometers east of the Goascoran River, which

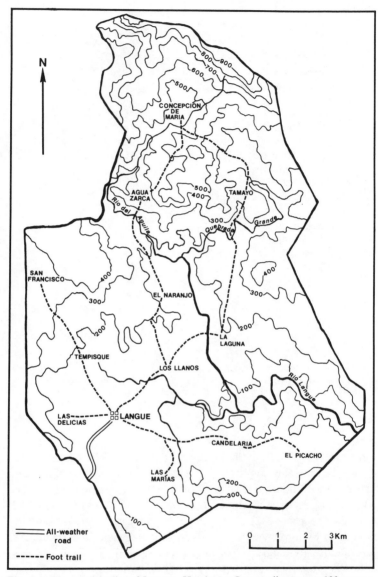

Fig. 5.1. The municipality of Langue, Honduras. Contour lines every 100 meters.

T A B L E 5.3 *Population of Langue, 1895–1974*

Year	Population	Average annual growth rate in the interval		Implied annual rate of migration
		Langue	National	
1895	3,475			
		1.71%	2.23%	− 0.52%
1930	6,241			
		2.08	2.39	− 0.31
1950	9,410			
		2.66	3.00	− 0.34
1961	12,508			
		0.45	2.70	− 2.52[a]
1974	13,252			

SOURCE: HDGEC 1932, 1952, 1964a, 1977.
[a]Includes out-migration of Salvadorean families.

demarcates the border between Honduras and El Salvador. The municipality covers about 139 square kilometers, divided about half and half between the valley and plains of the Langue River and its feeder streams in the south and the hilly to mountainous terrain in the north (see Fig. 5.1). The area is fairly described as tropical deciduous forest lifezone, though little forest remains (OAS 1963). According to soil studies, only the moderately fertile clay soil of the valley and plains is suitable for farming and grazing. The rest of the municipality has been pronounced unsuitable for anything but pine forests because of the steep hills and acid soil. Nevertheless, bush-fallow agriculture (described, for example, in Boserup 1965) is practiced throughout Langue on slopes as great as 60 degrees. In 1966, more than 41 percent of the area was in farms, approximately twice the national proportion (HDGEC 1968). On the average the area receives between 1,600 and 1,800 mm of rainfall, 85 percent of it concentrated in the rainy season between May and October.

According to preliminary figures from the 1974 census, Langue has about 13,000 inhabitants, of whom 2,400 (18.5 percent) live in the main village. The rest are divided among six rural hamlets (*aldeas*) and numerous smaller settlements called *caseríos*. This is about the same rural-urban distribution as in Tenancingo. Langue has about 3,000 more people than Tenancingo, but since it also incorporates much more land, its population density is far lower (95.3 people per square kilometer, compared with 189.2). Nevertheless, this is a very high figure for Honduras– over four times the national average.

Table 5.3 shows Langue's population and growth figures for the period 1895–1974. The growth rates are slightly but consistently below the national average, suggesting that there has long been some net out-migration from the area. Except for the intercensal period 1961–74 (which includes the departure of Langue's Salvadorean immigrants), the implied migration rates are much lower than Tenancingo's (Table 3.2).

The village of Langue, like Tenancingo, shows a clear Spanish colonial influence; but it is much more spread out and much less prosperous. The houses are arranged in loose rectangular blocks around a Catholic church (built in 1804) and central plaza. Few are white-washed, and none of the streets are paved or even set in cobblestone. What new buildings there are all house state or municipal agencies and institutions: a town hall, an office of the national malaria control program, a health center (opened in 1970), a telephone and telegraph office, two primary schools, a consolidated secondary school, and a small army post. As the market center for the surrounding area, the village also has a large municipal market building plus some 45 commercial establishments, including two pharmacies, two dry-goods stores, and several family-operated tiendas. Thanks to a Peace Corps project completed in 1968, the villagers have access to running water three hours a day, supplied through several public faucets. The village has also had intermittent electrical power in the evening hours since 1967. Neither of these services is available in the rural areas. A ten-kilometer all-weather road, built between 1960 and 1963, links up with the Pan-American Highway to the southwest, giving the village easy access to the capital city of Tegucigalpa some 100 kilometers away. Until 1965, when regular bus service was initiated, the principal means of transport were mules and ox-carts. Only one of the aldeas (Candelaria) is accessible by four-wheel drive vehicle. The others are connected to the village and to each other by footpaths, some of which double as ox-cart trails (see Fig. 5.1).

Two aspects of Langue's history are particularly important for this study. One is the early establishment of haciendas in the area. According to public documents in Langue, a Church official named Padre Fabián Flores de Banegas was granted title to a tract of six caballerías and four *cuerdas* (about 280 hectares) in 1668. This tract, the Hacienda Nuestra Señora de Candelaria, included most of the fertile valley of the Langue River and was centered in the spot where the aldea of the same name stands today. The hacienda changed hands several times in the 1700's and 1800's, and its boundaries were occasionally altered—pretty much as the owner pleased, according to municipal records. In 1849, in one such exchange, only four of the original six-plus caballerías were sold. Legal titles for the hacienda thereafter state that it consisted of four caballerías until, in 1890, the limits were arbitrarily extended by a local official even beyond their original dimensions. In 1895, when a purchaser asked the president of the Republic to renew his "primitive" title, the hacienda was legally recognized as incorporating the original six caballerías and four cuerdas. This owner later divided the hacienda among his grandchildren.

According to local tradition, the hacienda has been used over the years primarily for cattle grazing and the production of sugarcane. In earlier times, sugar was the more important of the two. A large sugar mill near the caserío Las Marías ran day and night during the harvest months preparing unrefined brown sugar (*panela*) for the Tegucigalpa market. As time went on, however, the growth of the population in the surrounding area, plus the mill's own heavy demand for fuel, saw more and more of Langue's forest cover cleared for hillside farm plots or for firewood. As a result, by 1900 firewood had become very scarce. Without fuel, the owner of the hacienda had no choice but to reduce sugar production (sugar continued to be produced in the mountain valleys of Tamayo and Concepción de María until the early 1930's, when the shortage of fuel closed the mills there as well). The obvious alternative was to make ranching the primary activity, and according to informants, the hacienda's cattle herd has grown steadily in the last 50 years. Judging from the distribution and abundance of thorny shrubs in the area today (mostly *espino blanco* [*Acacia farnesiana*] and *carbon blanco* [*Acacia pennulata*]), the valley has been extensively grazed for many years.

La Candelaria was not the only hacienda in the area. Indeed, all the best land in the surrounding countryside, except for the relatively flat and fertile area between Langue and Los Llanos (the plains), was incorporated into three large estates by 1800: Hacienda Sonare, on the municipality's southern border, Hacienda San Antonio on the eastern border, and Hacienda San José to the northeast, adjacent to Tamayo. These estates reportedly produced indigo, as well as cattle and sugarcane, in the early years. The ruins of processing plants can still be found in several places within Langue's boundaries.

The village of Langue in the Department of Valle, Honduras.

One of the main streets of the village.

The house of a tenant farmer in Langue. This family, unlike most, has no animals, fruit or shade trees, or garden plots.

One of the ejidatario *families interviewed in the study.*

Peasant families trek as much as 10 kilometers with their baskets and bundles of produce to buy and sell in the weekly market in Langue.

In hilly areas, a digging stick is used to prepare holes for the seeds, in this case grains of sorghum (from gourds tied to the farmer's waist). Last year's field, now being returned to fallow, can be seen on the opposite hill. The field of brush next to it, fallowed earlier, will be cleared for planting in a few years' time.

Fallow fields in Langue are usually burned at the end of the dry season just prior to planting. According to informants, the burn helps to clear the thorny vegetation, to control insect infestations, and to reduce the number of weed seeds.

Erosion commonly follows deforestation in the mountains of western Honduras, contributing greatly to the scarcity of arable land.

Nothing can be grown in the rocky substrates of family plots like this, though they are often included as "farms" in Honduran agricultural censuses.

Fences to exclude cattle from cropland areas are often constructed of second-growth trunks cut at the end of the fallow period. This field has been burned clean and now awaits spring rains and planting. Soil erosion is a common problem on such plots.

These haciendas influenced the human ecology of the area in two important ways. First, they tied Langue to the national economy early in the colonial period, so that it would be difficult to claim that interaction with outsiders was something new to the area. Second, the formation of the haciendas resulted in the competitive exclusion of the majority of the local population from the area's most productive agricultural resources. To be sure, numbers of local residents did cultivate small plots on hacienda properties, but this was allowed only in return for work performed for the owner or for rental payments. In consequence, as the population grew, the majority of Langue's farmers were forced ever farther inland and upland. In short, the poor soils and steep eroded hillsides farmed in Langue today have been under cultivation for many years. I saw no virgin forest of any description in the area, save for some pine along the ridge tops in the northern part of the municipality.

Fortunately for the inhabitants of Langue, the rapidly expanding haciendas were prevented from absorbing all the land within the present borders. In 1723, *los Indios de Langue* petitioned the colonial government for title to 12 caballerías and 13 cuerdas (over 540 hectares). Their petition was granted, giving them an ejido title to virtually all of the remaining non-hacienda land in the relatively fertile southern half of the municipality. Later, sizable portions of the northern part were brought under ejidal title as well. In contrast to the Salvadorean experience, these ejidal grants were preserved and even extended under the Republic.* Small-farmer agriculture persists in the area today thanks largely to the ejidal form of land tenure, which has protected peasants' claims to the land.

The second important aspect of Langue's economic history is a more recent development. Until World War II, the major ox-cart track and overland route in southern Honduras passed through the municipality. According to local informants, the town of Langue had played an important role in the trade between the tobacco-, indigo-, and coffee-producing areas in the mountains to the north and the salt-producing areas on the southern coast. Indeed, some claim that all of Tegucigalpa's salt was formerly purchased in Langue. The construction of the Pan-American Highway put an end to all this. Though

---

* In 1952 the census reported 343 farms operating on 2,096 hectares of ejidal land.

initially proposed to run through the municipality, the highway was finally routed well to the south, passing through the city of Nacaome. Langue's prosperity was further reduced when neighboring municipalities to the north acquired their own direct routes to the highway. By 1960 Langue's sales to Tegucigalpa were reduced to cattle, pigs, and a small amount of sesame grown on the larger farms.

To conclude, Langue, like Tenancingo, can be described as an "open" peasant community. The language of its inhabitants, together with their clothing, religious observances, and involvement with the national market (if recently reduced) all attest to a very "open" orientation to the outside world. There is no discernible vestige of any indigenous corporate structure among the inhabitants: families cultivate individual plots that they own, rent, or sharecrop; and even their access to public ejidal lands is regulated by state-appointed municipal officials. In this respect, as in others, Langue is representative of the small-farmer communities of the western and southern departments of Honduras.

Survey Results

My household survey in Langue was different in several respects from the earlier Tenancingo survey. Since my primary concern now was to obtain detailed information about the productivity of the peasants' holdings, and also as accurate an appraisal as possible of the land use of the Salvadorean immigrant families before they left in 1969, rather than to gather demographic data, it seemed clearly more appropriate to interview adult males. Accordingly, the study was timed to coincide with the end of the dry season (April– May 1976), a period when the men would not be engaged in time-absorbing agricultural pursuits. The questionnaire from the Tenancingo study was modified to include new questions on crop rotation, yields, and weed and pest problems, and on the land holdings of the Salvadorean families of Langue in the pre-1969 years (see Appendix B). In addition, I decided to set the age limits for potential respondents at 30 to 75 years (i.e., older than in Tenancingo), since in rural areas males commonly marry at an older age than females.

Four Honduran students from the National University, all with previous interviewing experience, assisted with the collection of data.

The interviews were again conducted with a hamlet-stratified random sample of households. Detailed local maps from 1974, complete with house numbers, were available from the Census Bureau for three of the aldeas. Maps for two other hamlets were drawn up and numbered in a similar fashion. Because of the distance to the sixth aldea, Concepción de María (a five-hour journey each way by mule) we did not prepare a map in advance, but simply interviewed at every fourth house as we worked our way along.

In all, we visited 190 of the 751 houses in the total subset of caseríos sampled. From these we obtained 165 complete interviews, with only two refusals (1.2 percent). In the other cases the men were either ill, outside our age limits, or away from the hamlet for the day. The sample accordingly represents 22 percent of the families in the study area, a figure that is comparable to the sample obtained in Tenancingo. As before, these data were coded, keypunched, and computer-analyzed using MIDAS at the University of Michigan.

The Langue and Tenancingo sample populations are very much alike in some respects. For example, 36.5 percent of the Langue sample lives in palm-thatched chozas, compared with 33.4 percent in Tenancingo. The rest live in wattle-and-daub or adobe houses with clay tile roofs.

Only 14 of the men interviewed (8.5 percent) were born outside of Langue. The same was true for 24 of 158 spouses included in the sample (15.2 percent), although many of these had moved from adjacent rural areas at the time of their marriage. The latter figure is very similar to the proportion of females born outside Tenancingo.

The median age of marriage to current spouses is 24 for the men and 19 for the women (compared with 26 and 21 in Tenancingo). Seventy-five men are legally married to their present wives in a church ceremony (45.5 percent), and 76 (46.1 percent) are acompañado. Five men are separated, five are single, and four are widowers. Illiteracy is 72.6 percent among males and 73.1 percent among females—considerably higher than in Tenancingo in both cases.

The average age of the respondents is 46.5 years. A chi-square test comparing this age distribution with the distribution among all rural men over 30 in the municipality was insignificant at the 0.05 level. The sample can therefore be considered representative in this respect.

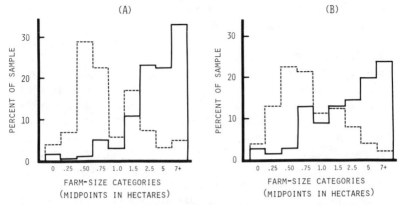

Fig. 5.2. Changes in the distribution of farmland between generations in Langue. Diagram A shows the access to land reported for the past generation (fathers of the respondents; N = 120), and Diagram B shows access to land in the present generation (respondents themselves in 1976; N = 147). The figures are based on data for all farm plots, regardless of tenure. The dashed curves are from the analogous figure for Tenancingo (Fig. 3.3).

Changes in the Land Base Between Generations

Figure 5.2 compares the land base of the present and past generations in Langue (respondents and their fathers). Whereas the fathers had access to an average of 6.51 hectares, their sons have access to only 4.59 hectares. The difference, a decrease of 29.6 percent between the generations, is significant at the 0.01 level ($t = 2.56$). In large part, the decrease is due to the greatly increased numbers of families with plots of 1.0 hectare or less (28.5 percent, compared with 10.8 percent). A difference is also apparent in the maximum sizes of the farms reported for the two generations, with the range reaching 75 hectares for the fathers, compared with a maximum of only 47 hectares for the sons.

For comparison, the figure includes the distributions obtained in Tenancingo for roughly comparable generations. As expected, large and statistically significant differences were obtained. The average for the present generation in Tenancingo (1.10 hectares) is only 24.0 percent of the Langue figure. Thus, despite the significant shrinkage in the land base between the generations *and* the yield differential discussed above, the aggregate land base of small farmers is appreciably larger in Langue than in Tenancingo.

Other information from the survey suggests that the land base in Langue is also more secure. For example, almost twice as many families in Langue own at least some part of their land as in Tenancingo (72.1 percent, compared with 43.4 percent). Much of this difference is attributable to the persistence of ejidal lands. Since families have traditionally controlled inheritance rights to ejidal plots, these plots are often regarded as "owned" by those who use them. As might be expected, the percentage of families dependent on rental lands in Langue is also lower than in Tenancingo (39.4 percent, compared with 46.1 percent). In addition, the rental period is generally longer: a median of two years in Langue, compared with one year in Tenancingo. Several families claim to have had continuous rental agreements for more than ten years.

A slightly higher proportion of the men in Langue inherited land from their fathers: 28.5 percent, compared with 23.6 percent in Tenancingo. On the other hand, the incidence of such inheritances by women is considerably lower than in Tenancingo (7.3 percent in Langue, compared with 15.1 percent), though this figure may have been biased by the interview procedure. A substantial number of families have acquired land on their own; 51 families (30.9 percent) had purchased titles or use rights to a plot of land, and seven others (4.2 percent) had obtained ejidal grants from the municipality. Ten families (6.1 percent) say they are working land as squatters.

Earlier in this chapter, it was hypothesized that small farmers in Honduras would be more affected by competitive losses than the large farmers. At the national level, the data suggest that small farmers are forced by the size of their holdings to farm their plots year after year. In contrast, large farmers can afford the long fallow period (seven–ten years) required for the maximum fertility of their land. To see if this was the case in Langue, I performed a piecewise regression analysis to examine the relationship between farm size and land use. More specifically, the regression was used to relate the average amount of land a family had used for the production of food crops over the past four years to its average holdings over the same period. To show nonlinear changes in the relationship, I made separate analyses for farms averaging 0.1–1.7 hectares, 1.7–5.0 hectares, and 5.0 hectares or more.

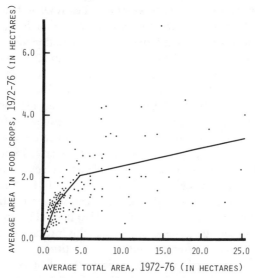

Fig. 5.3. Average land in food crops as a function of farm size for a four-year period in Langue. The curve represents a piece-wise linear regression of the data for individual families (dots) over the period.

The results are shown in Figure 5.3. Regression equations for the smallest and largest categories of farms reveal in both cases a statistically significant trend of increasing food-crop area with farm size.* However, the slopes are drastically different. The smallest farms, on average, had 90 percent of their land in food crops for four straight years, whereas the large farms put a constant 1.83 hectares plus only 6 percent of their land into food crops in that period.

These results suggest an important differential in sensitivity to potential competitors. Below a farm size of about 2.0 hectares, peasant

---

* Defining the predicted average area in food crops as F_p and the average total area as T, for the farms of 0.1–1.7 hectare

$$F_p = 0.08 + 0.90(T). \quad R^2 = 0.668. \quad F = 90.5. \quad p < 0.01,$$
$$ (.11) \quad (.09) \quad \text{(standard error)}$$

and for the farms of 5.0 hectares or more

$$F_p = 1.83 + 0.06(T). \quad R^2 = 0.071. \quad F = 4.3. \quad p < 0.05.$$
$$ (.48) \quad (.03) \quad \text{(standard error)}$$

families apparently find it necessary to use nearly all of their land every year for food crops. For such families, any reduction in land availability would mean a reduction in food-crop production and therefore in the family food supply. Families with more than 5.0 hectares, on the other hand, appear to be under little pressure to use their plots intensively. A small reduction in the land area available to these families would not necessarily affect their food production and supply, though it would of course reduce the amount of time they could afford to leave land fallow. In a related finding, the numbers of cattle raised by farmers shows a direct and rapid increase with farm size, going from zero on all farms under 0.50 hectare to more than ten on every farm over 25 hectares (correlation coefficient $= 0.66$, $p < .0001$). A reduction of land on the larger farms might instead mean some reduction in marketable production. In short, Figure 5.3 supports the hypothesis that the small farmers in Langue are in a highly precarious position in terms of the possible effects of outside competition.

The data I gathered on yields indicate that their position is even more precarious than the figure implies. Farmers were asked to describe their normal yields year by year for the first four years after bringing a plot out of fallow. A comparison of the yields reported by farmers in the same two categories (i.e., those with 0.1–1.7 hectares and those with 5.0 hectares or more) reveals not only that small farmers initially harvest less per unit of land than the large farmers, but also that the difference between the returns increases over the course of four growing seasons. Their first-year yields of maize and sorghum grown together averaged only 1,404 kilograms per hectare, compared with the large farms' 2,493 kilograms. The difference was significant at the 0.0001 level ($t = -5.7$). In that year, the yields of small farmers were 56.3 percent of the yields on the large farms. In subsequent years the gap in productivity widened, with the small farms' yields dropping to 46.5 percent of the large farms' in year 2, to 38.9 percent in year 3, and to 16.6 percent in year 4. By the third year, the small farms' combined yields averaged only 455 kilograms per hectare, compared with 1,170 kilograms on the larger ones. A majority of the small farmers claimed that any planting beyond that year was useless. Many of the larger farmers, however, said their land could fruitfully be exploited for 15 consecutive years. All but two of these farms, it should be noted, were situated in the fertile valley lands of the Langue River.

It can therefore be concluded that the food production of small farmers is sharply constrained by their access to land. The evidence suggests that the *potential* for food-crop production grows exponentially with farm size. The *realized* production, on the other hand, grows in more of an S-shaped fashion. At about 2.0 hectares a plateau is reached where it appears that family food requirements are relatively easily met. Above 2.0 hectares, additional land can either be left fallow for longer periods to maintain high yields or used for cattle production or commercial crops.

Family Income

Given this knowledge of land-use practices and yields in Langue, we would expect to find agriculturally derived income growing in a nonlinear fashion over the range of farm sizes—just as we did in Tenancingo, though there the situation was complicated by the ubiquitous production of palm trenzas.

Figures 5.4 and 5.5 summarize the family income data from the Langue sample. As in Tenancingo, the distribution approximates log-normal (the scale is roughly comparable to the Tenancingo plot in Fig. 3.4). In contrast to Tenancingo, however, more than a fifth of the Langue families have no cash income at all. The median monthly income is also lower (U.S. $5.00–$10.00, compared with $8.00–$12.00). A distributional tail of high monthly incomes was found; in most cases, that income derived from cattle and hog raising.

The relationship between farm size and average monthly income is

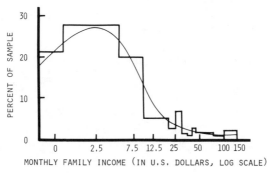

Fig. 5.4. Monthly family income in Langue. Based on data for the full sample population (N = 165).

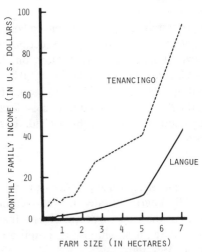

Fig. 5.5. Relationship between monthly family income and land base in Langue. Based on data for the families in which the men work only on the family plot (N = 81).

shown in Figure 5.5. As expected, the relationship is nonlinear and nearly exponential. In addition, income grows rapidly only above 2.0 hectares, consistent with the analysis above. A simple one-way variance test confirmed that this trend is significant, despite within-group variance, at the 0.01 level (F-statistic = 5.67). Figure 5.5 also shows the Tenancingo income curve for comparison. The curves are similar, but Tenancingo's is substantially higher. The data for the farm sizes below 1.5 hectares suggest that much of this difference is indeed attributable to the lack of a cash-producing handicraft in Langue comparable to the palm braids of Tenancingo.

Relationship Between Child Mortality and Farm Size

To this point, the Langue data suggest that the scarcity of land for small farmers affects both their ability to produce food for their families and their ability to earn supplemental cash incomes. Both of these can be expected to influence the family's diet and health. Accordingly, we might reasonably expect to find land availability strongly influencing the peasant's ability to survive and reproduce here, just as we did

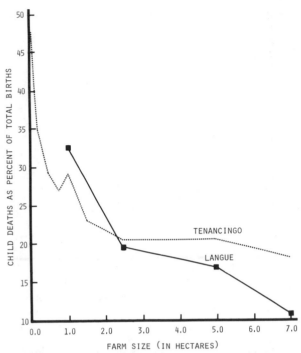

Fig. 5.6. Child mortality by farm size in the past generation of landowners in Langue. Data are for females born between 1876 and 1930.

for Tenancingo. As before, let us use the data on child mortality to test this hypothesis.

Figure 5.6 shows the child mortality in the past generation in Langue—i.e., among those of the respondents' parents who (1) owned some amount of land and (2) had birth dates within the same range of years as the past generation in Tenancingo. This leaves a subset of 60 families, with 500 births and 84 child deaths, for an average mortality of 16.8 percent—a considerable decrease from the average for the same generation of owners in Tenancingo (26.2 percent).

However, as we see in the figure, the position and shape of the two curves are similar. Total child mortality in Langue drops from 32.6 percent among the families with less than 1.5 hectares to 10.5 percent

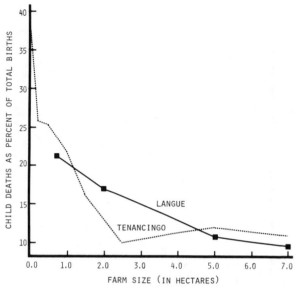

Fig. 5.7. Child mortality by farm size in the present generation of landowners in Langue. The present generation covers the 1920–45 female birth cohorts.

among the families with 7.0 hectares or more. The lower average mortality reported here may be the product of land distribution, since there were no landless families in this subsample, and it included 22 families with 7.0+ hectares of land, compared with just eight families with that much land in Tenancingo's past generation group.

Figure 5.7 compares the mortality curves among children of the present generation of landowners in Langue and Tenancingo. The Langue plot is based on 70 mothers in the same birth cohorts as in the El Salvador study. Though the Langue curve is not quite as steep as Tenancingo's and the average rate of mortality is lower (12.7 percent, compared with 21.0 percent), the general trend is qualitatively similar.

In order to control for the effects of distributional differences between the Langue and Tenancingo samples, I used the same log-linear regression model on the Langue data as before (see p. 92). If the land base has had a similar influence on mortality in the two areas, we would expect to see a similarity in the land area regression coefficients.

T A B L E 5.4   *Regression Analysis of Child Mortality in the Past and Present Generations of the Langue Sample*

Source of mortality data	Constant		Total number of births, B, in family		Natural-logged land area, L, used by family	
	Regression coefficient	Statistic	Regression coefficient	Statistic	Regression coefficient	Statistic
Past generation						
$(N = 112)^a$	$-0.12(C')$		$0.33(C'')$		$-0.26(C''')$	
Standard error		0.53		0.04		0.11
t-statistic		-0.22		7.95		-2.28
Significance		n.s.		0.0001		0.02
Partial correlation		—		0.61		-0.21
Present generation						
$(N = 135)^b$	$0.74(C')$		$0.24(C'')$		$-0.35(C''')$	
Standard error		0.38		0.03		0.09
t-statistic		1.97		7.60		-3.61
Significance		n.s.		0.0001		0.0001
Partial correlation		—		0.55		-0.30

NOTE: The regression model predicts the number of child deaths, D, in a family according to the formula $D = C' + C''(B) + C'''(L)$.
[a] $R^2 = 0.37$. Multiple R $= 0.61$. F-statistic $= 32.3$. $p < .0001$.
[b] $R^2 = 0.31$. Multiple R $= 0.56$. F-statistic $= 30.7$. $p < .0001$.

As in the Tenancingo study, the regression covered all the families that work land for themselves, regardless of tenure. The results are given in Table 5.4.

Comparing these results with those obtained in Tenancingo (see Table 3.6), we find that the Langue C'' coefficient of child deaths as a function of total births is lower for both generations (0.33, compared with 0.49, for the past generation; 0.24, compared with 0.36, for the present generation). Though better sanitation or nutrition could account for this difference, it is more likely the result of underreporting by the male respondents. That would be consistent with the relatively high unexplained variance in the Langue analyses. In contrast to values of 0.48 and 0.49 in Tenancingo, the R^2 values here are 0.37 and 0.31.

Whatever the reason for the disparity, the land base–child mortality results for the two communities are remarkably similar. In both cases the present generation shows a higher C''' coefficient than the past generation, and in both cases the slopes are very similar (-0.26 in

Langue and −0.28 in Tenancingo for the past generation; −0.35 versus −0.37 for the present generation). Despite some apparent differences in the quality of the data, we can conclude that the relationship between land scarcity and child mortality is qualitatively and quantitatively similar in Langue and Tenancingo. If these data are accurate in suggesting a lower average rate of mortality in Langue, we know at least that the difference is not due to any direct influence of the land base. The relationship between scarcity and survival suggested here is fundamentally the same in both cases.

Salvadorean Immigrants

To this point, the analysis of survey data from Langue has shown not only that land is scarce for small farmers in the municipality, but also that they are in a very precarious position with respect to competitive losses. Many of the poorer families in the area have depended on rented plots all their lives. As indicated earlier, many others (30.9 percent) have purchased title or use rights to the land they are now farming. Given an appreciable in-migration of landless and land-poor Salvadoreans in the years after World War II, I hypothesized, the landless and land-poor of Langue were likely to be the most affected. In response to my questions about the Salvadorean immigrants, I expected two kinds of answers: expressions of hostility indicative of a competitive relationship; and accounts of the local peasants' participation in getting the Salvadoreans expelled from the community. In order not to bias the results in favor of this hypothesis, I did not tell my research assistants of this expectation. This section describes the information obtained concerning the immigrants' use of land in Langue and their interactions with the Honduran residents. Because the respondents' descriptions of Salvadorean families were often redundant, the data had to be compiled by caserío and checked for consistency. In cases of discrepancies, I have used the consensus in the analysis.

According to my respondents, 65 Salvadorean families had lived in the study area in 1969. This represents 8.8 percent of the estimated 740 households in the area at the time. The first of these families had come to Langue in 1914, and more than half of them had settled there by 1950. At the time of their expulsion, these families were farming

207.5 manzanas of land, or 145.0 hectares. This represents 4.3 percent of the total farmland in the area, judging from the survey results, and works out to an average of 2.23 hectares per family, or roughly one-half of the estimated average for the Honduran inhabitants in 1975. Among the Salvadorean families there were 24 landowners (37 percent), controlling 110.0 manzanas, or an average of 4.5 hectares apiece. This figure is close to the average for the Langue sample reported above (4.59 hectares), but that average, as we have seen, is far below the Honduran national average of 13.6 hectares in 1966. The other 41 families rented or sharecropped an average of 0.86 hectare, a figure that puts most of the immigrants squarely in the ranks of the land-poor. The total area rented and sharecropped by these families, 35.3 hectares, represents about 10 percent of the land in those forms of tenure in 1969.

The vast majority of the Salvadoreans lived in the relatively fertile southern half of the municipality, including 25 of the renter-share-cropper families (or 59 percent of that group) in the aldea of Candelaria alone. Most of these families had worked for many years on the hacienda in return for the use of a small subsistence plot. Several caseríos in the steep and rocky northern areas reported no Salvadorean immigrants at all.

To sum up: the Salvadorean immigrants who came to Langue before 1969 were concentrated in the areas of flattest and best soil; accounted for 8.8 percent of the families in the study area; were mostly renters or sharecroppers; and held about 10 percent of all the rented lands in the community. Although the Honduran census's national total for the Salvadoreans resident in Honduras in 1950 is unreliable for the reasons discussed in Chapter Two, the figures for Langue seem to me both reasonable and not exaggerated, as they are for many areas. For example, the census reported that in 1950 Langue had 32 adult male immigrants (49 percent of the total figure I obtained), which accords well with my respondents' reports that half the Salvadoreans had settled in Langue by that time. The census further reported that only 5.1 percent of all the Salvadorean immigrants in the department of Valle lived in Langue, which then had 14.4 percent of the department's general population.

To this point, the survey data are consistent with my hypothesis: the Salvadoreans posed the greatest competitive threat in the category of

rented lands. However, the reaction of the community to their presence and particularly the reaction of the Honduran renters and sharecroppers was not as expected. The vast majority of the respondents
expressed no hostility toward the Salvadoreans; and even more surprisingly, the renter-sharecroppers seemed to be the least concerned.
Here are some typical responses to the question "How were your
relations with these families?":

Renter of 2 manzanas: "Between us the relations were good because they are
good people. They behaved very properly."

Renter of 1 manzana: "A neighboring family of Salvadoreans rented one
manzana as well, but they left with the war. Our relations were pretty good."

Renter of 1 manzana: "Nearby there were six families. They never bothered
anybody."

Owner of 2 manzanas: "There were three families in this caserío with a good
deal of land between them. The authorities came and removed them before
the war without much trouble. They weren't enemies of the people here."

As it turned out, the most openly hostile views were expressed by a
few of the wealthier landowners:

Owner of 20 manzanas: "It's all right with me if they never come
back—they are thieves and nasty people."

Owner of 10 manzanas: "I don't want them to be allowed back in [to
Honduras] because there would then be fights between Salvadoreans and
Hondurans when they return to claim the lands they left behind."

Again contrary to my expectations, the local residents were apparently never active or indeed in any way involved in the expulsion of the
immigrants. In every case of forced removal described to us in the
course of the survey, the proceedings were handled by outside "authorities," including army officials.

Despite the precariousness of family livelihood among the smallest
farmers in Langue, then, there is little evidence of any hostility on
their part toward the Salvadorean immigrants. Why this should be
the case is suggested by another surprising finding. According to the
survey results, the immigrants actually had very little effect on the
availability of land to Langue's renters and sharecroppers. Families
that have rented or sharecropped in Langue since 1966 claim to have
had nearly as much land then (0.78 hectare per family) as in 1971 (0.80
hectare per family). A t-statistic of 0.23 indicates that the difference is
insignificant at the .05 level. In other words, the 41 Salvadorean fami-

lies that rented and sharecropped in the area before the Soccer War obtained land without significantly affecting the land available to their Honduran counterparts. This suggests that land scarcity for farmers in these categories was not a density-dependent phenomenon, but one controlled by other factors. The Salvadorean immigrants and the landless and land-poor of Langue appear not to have been direct competitors, as originally hypothesized.

Agrarian Conflict in Langue, 1955–1965

It seems clear, however, that the Salvadorean immigrants did exacerbate competitive interactions on a different level. At the start of this chapter I described the early history of the haciendas in the Langue area, and how they came to occupy much of the best land in the municipality. The more recent history of one particular hacienda, La Candelaria, is important to an understanding of the land dynamics of the community since 1900.

On the death of the widow who managed the hacienda from 1912 to 1930, the lands were divided among various grandchildren, according to the terms of her will. In 1931, the husband of one of these heirs—hereafter called the hacendado—began to raise cattle on his wife's portion of the estate. Because of the length and severity of the dry season in the area, cattle must be grazed over an unusually broad expanse of pasture, and it was not long before the hacendado began to increase his holdings. According to municipal records, he first bought an additional portion of the estate from one of his wife's sisters in 1931. Then, as several informants put it, during the next decade, while the hacendado was also Langue's mayor, *"nieto por nieto se fue comprando"* (grandchild by grandchild he set about buying Candelaria lands). By the early years of World War II, he had expanded his operations to the point where he had his own bull and a breeding herd of about 30 cows. In those days the hacienda also had about 200 colono families (i.e., workers who paid for use rights to small family plots). According to informants, in 1950 17 of these families were Salvadorean immigrants.

After World War II, with the completion of the Pan-American Highway and a favorable market for beef, the hacendado renewed his efforts to expand both his herd and his grazing lands. According to informants, three important events took place in 1955. First, the hacendado added 50 cows to his breeding stock (purchased from a son who had a ranch to the east). Second, the same bank loan that financed the expansion of the herd provided for the purchase of large amounts of barbed wire used to fence in new areas of pasture. Part of the fenced area included the homesites of ten colono families, which were then promptly evicted from hacienda lands. Third, the hacendado began to install fences near the caserío El Picacho (see Fig. 5.1), on what local residents had long considered national lands (*baldío*). According to municipal records, he bought out a sister-in-law at about this time to add the last outstanding portion of the original hacienda to his holdings. However, the documents for that transaction refer to the "uncertain" boundaries of the property, and the title lays claim to the entire southern half of the Langue valley, including the area of national lands. According to the well-defined boundaries in the various title documents dating back to 1668, the hacienda at its largest had included only a small part of this land.

Soon after, the hacendado circulated a legal petition among the residents of El Picacho asking them to recognize him as the legal owner of the full area. According to informants, more than 1,000 signatures or X's were obtained from the campesinos. Nearly all illiterate, they were told that the petition was a statement guaranteeing their rights.

But they learned their mistake soon enough, and within a year an organization called Los Baldíos had been formed to resist the hacendado's continuing encroachments. The group, made up primarily of colonos on the hacienda and small farmers living on the national lands of El Picacho, reportedly had 100 member families, including four of the 17 Salvadorean colonos. The rest of the people involved, including the other Salvadoreans, were too frightened to join, according to informants—and with good reason. A large band of men, all local residents affected by the encroachments, cut the hacienda's barbed wire fences one moonless night shortly after the formation of Los Baldíos, allowing the cattle herd to escape. Soldiers appeared early the next morning and took five of the men off to the jail in Nacaome.

Undeterred, the group cut the fences a second and then a third time, at which point the hacendado hired 50 armed guards to patrol the boundaries of the estate day and night, and had 40 members of Los

Baldíos imprisoned as suspects. One former colono-respondent, whose four manzanas had been fenced in by the hacendado in 1955, remarked, "We only survived because the people were organized and we found a sympathetic lawyer."

The "sympathetic lawyer," a man from Nacaome, arranged the release of the prisoners and then checked the title records in the National Archives. He also hired an agronomist to clarify the boundary problem. The agronomist's final report, on file with other public documents in Langue, certifies that a wedge-shaped piece of national land covering nearly 2,000 hectares had indeed been illegally declared to fall within the property limits of La Candelaria. The report nicely corroborates the story repeated to me by informants from the area.

In the end, the hacendado lost not only his claim to the land around El Picacho, but also most of his assets, including the cattle. In addition, he lost a total of eight years of payments from colonos and renters, another action sponsored by Los Baldíos (users had been required to pay him 12 lempiras — U.S. $6.00 — per manzana per growing season, or 480 pounds of loose grain). He apparently declared bankruptcy, turned his land titles over to the National Agricultural Bank, and moved away. In 1965, the bank gave the lands to the National Agrarian Institute. Since 1967 they have been farmed by an agricultural cooperative, La Estrella Langueña (The Star of Langue), organized by the INA and composed of the former renters, sharecroppers, and colonos of La Candelaria. Because of the legal prohibition against foreigners working on any lands included in agrarian reform projects, the immigrant families in the area were excluded from the cooperative. All were finally expelled, of course, in 1969.

Conclusions

It is clear that the in-migration of substantial numbers of Salvadoreans did not have a major competitive effect on the availability of lands for the small farmers of Langue. As we have seen, the poorer Hondurans did not experience any significant reduction of their land base even after the majority of Salvadoreans had arrived. Despite the relatively precarious resource base of these families, the evidence does not allow a rejection of the null hypothesis.

The lack of a major competitive effect can largly be explained by the fact that most of the immigrants were tenants. In Langue the availability of lands for tenants was influenced more by the land-use decisions of large landowners than by an expansion in the numbers of workers seeking places as renters, sharecroppers, or colonos. The landowners of Langue, including the hacendado, reportedly welcomed the Salvadoreans' solicitations for tenancy rights because of their reputation as hard workers. Until the cattle market made that form of land use more profitable than farming, landowners accommodated the Salvadoreans in addition to (and not at the expense of) their traditional arrangements with Honduran residents.

As we have seen, far from threatening the position of the landless and land-poor of Langue, the Salvadorean immigrants eventually teamed up with them to destroy the land base of the largest landowner in the area. In short, nearly all the land-related hostilities in Langue before 1969 took place between the owner of Hacienda La Candelaria and the combined forces of the immigrant and resident poor peasants—not between the campesinos of different nationalities.

This chapter provides one example of the resource competition that took place between peasants and the estate owners in Honduras during the post–World War II expansion of commercial agriculture. This competition for land between peasants and hacendados is hardly a unique story—to Honduras or for that matter to other parts of Central America and Mexico at earlier periods (see Friedrich 1970; D. Browning 1971). As with these other cases, the conflict in Langue had an important land distribution component. It was clearly not a simple matter of a density-dependent change in resource scarcity.

CHAPTER SIX

Conclusion

In the last chapter we saw that the reason land became increasingly scarce for the small farmers of Langue was not the growth of the poor population or the competition of the Salvadorean immigrants, but rather the expansion of commercial agriculture by the largest land-owner in the area. But as we also saw, the peasants of Langue, particularly renters, sharecroppers and colonos, did not sit quietly by to let the lands they had worked for years slip into other hands; they not only organized but in the end successfully resisted the encroachment of the hacendado.

The experience in Langue was repeated in many parts of Honduras in the 1950's and 1960's (see, e.g., R. A. White 1972, 1977; Stares 1972; and K. H. Parsons 1976 on similar conflicts elsewhere in southern Honduras). And so, sometimes, was the outcome. In 1969, for example, after four years of failure to get governmental support, the peasants of Namasigue in Choluteca announced their intention to reoccupy an area of ejidal land near the village and plant crops. An assembly of campesinos resolved:

"We have waited sufficient time. Hunger obliges us to act since we have children to feed and women who do not even have anything to clothe themselves. We know that the lands of El Bosque, La Chorrea, and Las Minitas are common lands of Namasigue. We are all agreed on the necessities which are sapping our strength day by day and we no longer have a place to sow our subsistence crops. And our wives no longer have clothes to cover their flesh. On the following day we will occupy the neighboring lands of the municipality." They did, on August 25, 1969. They continued the occupancy of the land and planted their crops. The success was electrifying to the landless campesinos of the area. (R. A. White 1972: 847, cited in K. H. Parsons 1976: 16–17)

Similar events have been described for the communities of El Corpus, San Bernardo, and Monjaras (Capa & Stycos 1974: 115, 128; R. A.

White 1972: 181). In these areas, as in many others, hacendados had expanded their lands for cattle or cotton production at the direct expense of smallholders. And usually, as Parsons notes (1976: 16), the smallholders stoutly resisted: "In community after community the campesinos formed committees to defend and fight for what they considered to be the right to occupy their own lands."

Although it is impossible to determine how much land the Enclosure Movement involved, campesino reclamations (or land invasions as they were often termed in the press) became increasingly frequent in the years before the conflict with El Salvador.* The majority took place in the denser western and southern regions, but the north saw a fair share as well. In the Ulúa Valley on the north coast, for example, when the United Fruit Company abandoned a large tract because of crop failure, "campesinos invaded this land, claiming that it was available for settlement as national land under the terms of the Agrarian Reform Law of 1962–63; INA upheld the claims of the campesinos [and] not only sanctioned the occupation of the land but helped these workers organize themselves into a production cooperative for the growing of bananas and other fruits which were sold to the fruit company" (K. H. Parsons 1976: 18).

Like the hacendado of Langue, many of the large landowners responded to the campesinos' "invasions" with force. As the agency responsible for the distribution of national and ejidal lands, the INA was often called in to resolve disputes. As Kenneth Parsons notes (1976: 17), "This placed INA in the middle—petitioned by small farmers to validate their claim that the land was national land and therefore available for settlement, sanctioning their occupation of the

* But some indication of the magnitude of these changes can be gleaned from Honduran census data. For example, bearing in mind that many of the large landowners not only expelled peasant families from hacienda lands, but also appropriated to their own use sizable chunks of ejidal and national lands, we can take as an indicator the changes in farmland under non-property tenure (ejidal, national and ocupante lands) in this period. Considering first the national totals, we find that these lands declined by 68,751 hectares between 1952 and 1966—from 917,356 hectares to 848,605 (HDGEC 1954: 37, 1968: 27). But these figures mask the true picture because of an increase at the same time of 81,485 hectares in non-property lands in the low-density frontier settlement areas of Olancho, Gracias a Díos, El Paraiso, and Yoro. The seven departments where traditional agriculture was most concentrated (Choluteca, Copan, Lempira, Morazán, La Paz, Santa Barbara, and Valle) lost 145,549 hectares, or 32.3 percent of their non-property lands. This figure represents a change in land tenure on more than 11.1 percent of all the land in farms (1,309,000 hectares) in those areas.

land, and counter-petitioned by large landholders for an eviction on the basis that the land was rightfully theirs." According to the institute's *Memorias* for 1968, the INA mediated 68 such agrarian conflicts in that year alone.

Following a banana workers' strike on the north coast in 1954, what had once been the isolated actions of local resistance groups began to be transformed into a national campesino movement. By the late 1960's, most peasant groups sought the aid of one or another of the country's three peasant leagues or unions in their disputes with large landowners (see R. A. White 1977: 181). In the case of Hacienda San Bernardo described in Chapter Four, for example, the peasants called in the National Association of Honduran Peasants (ANACH) to help organize the occupation of the hacienda in April 1969 (Capa & Stycos 1974: 128). Another occupation in 1969, organized by the National Union of Campesinos (UNC), affected some 5,000 hectares of private property. That occupation, more than any other, in the judgment of a former INA director, "negated the old belief that a land problem existed only in El Salvador and not in Honduras" (Ponce 1974: 7).

The Role of the Salvadoreans in Honduran Agrarian Conflicts

The large landowners reacted to the increasing strength of the campesino organizations by forming an organization of their own — the National Federation of Agriculturalists and Cattle Ranchers of Honduras (FENAGH). This body, from its founding in 1966, issued a steady stream of petitions and letters designed to press the central government to take action against *las invasiones*. The President of the Republic was one of the main targets for this pressure campaign. In a petition dated November 24, 1967, for example, he was told: "The Federation condemns the invasion and usurpation of lands in Honduras, a procedure that, in its view, can in no way provide a legitimate basis for a true Agrarian Reform" (the petition is reproduced in Carías & Slutzky 1971: 128–34). The Federation went on to call for the restitution of all lands under legal title that had been seized by peasant groups and for a guarantee of the landowners' property rights in the future. Most important of all for this study, it was in this petition that FENAGH first singled out the Salvadorean immigrants as principals in the invasions:

This problem of land invasions and future land grants obliges the Federation to denounce before the President of the Republic that, in considerable number, it is foreigners who are usurping rural properties, especially foreigners of Salvadorean nationality.

FENAGH repeated this charge several times over the next few years. By June 26, 1969, in a public statement issued on the very eve of the Soccer War, it was prepared to assert, without any qualification, that "a majority of the land invasions have been made by foreigners" (the complete text of that statement is reprinted in Carías & Slutzky 1971: 135–38).

Much of FENAGH's pressure campaign was also directed at the INA. In the late 1960's it repeatedly accused the institute of encouraging the peasants to occupy private land in violation of the constitutional rights of property holders. These accusations stirred the INA into issuing a press release in reply: "The INA assures FENAGH that it does not permit, consent to, or stimulate peasant invasions of land belonging to members of FENAGH. FENAGH accusations to that effect are unfounded" (INA 1968: 37). But published assurances like this were apparently unconvincing to the large landholders, for in 1969 FENAGH filed a lawsuit against the director of the INA; the charge was that he had allowed the laws protecting private property to be violated (Alonso & Slutzky 1971: 287).

The INA's subsequent actions and other events of 1969 suggest how effective the FENAGH campaign was. In that year, the institute began several new agricultural settlement projects on areas of national land in Honduras. Hitherto the INA had largely ignored the 1962 law banning all but native-born Hondurans from these projects. But due largely to FENAGH arguments that "foreign usurpers" were a substantial part of the agrarian problem in Honduras, a new, "strictly nationalistic" policy was announced by INA Director Rigoberto Sandoval Corea. On May 3, 1969, he sent out letters to 57 Salvadorean families living on the site of a reform project at Guacamaya, in the department of Yoro, giving them 30 days to leave their homesteads on national lands (the letter is reproduced as an appendix in INA 1969). Soon thereafter, similar eviction notices were sent to Salvadorean residents in other areas of the country. At the end of the 30-day period, the Honduran army promptly set about enforcing these orders. On June 4, 1969, 54 of the 57 families were removed from Guacamaya (*El*

Cronista, Tegucigalpa, June 5, 1969; *El Día,* Tegucigalpa, June 5, 1969). What was described as "cleaning the area of *guanacos*" (a pejorative term for Salvadoreans) was then carried out in 18 other aldeas of Yoro (*El Cronista,* June 18, 1969).

As we have seen, these expulsions came at a time when the governments of El Salvador and Honduras were already in disagreement over what one analyst has termed the "unequal benefits" of the Central American Common Market agreement (Fagan 1970). To this point the grievances had principally come from the Honduran government, which felt its economy was victimized by regional trade patterns.* With the expulsions, however, the Salvadorean government also turned defensive, breaking diplomatic relations with Honduras on June 26, and filing a petition with the Inter-American Commission on Human Rights. The petition cited a wide range of abuses committed against Salvadoreans, including the forced removal of an estimated 500 families from their rural Honduran homesteads (Guerrero 1969).

There were, however, other causes for alarm among Salvadorean officials. As Frank Bachmura notes (1971: 285), El Salvador had benefited for many years from the gradual migration of 10 percent or more of its low-income inhabitants. As he puts it, "Reduced population pressure . . . eased political and economic development problems" that would otherwise have been considerably worse. But once the expulsion of migrants began, the Salvadorean government could plainly see the threat of having those benefits reversed all at once. Internal documents indicate that national advisors were greatly worried about the social and political consequences of great numbers of landless and unemployed refugees (CONAPLAN 1969).

By an unfortunate coincidence, the expulsions also began shortly before the soccer teams of the two countries met in the World Cup semi-final matches. With the defeat of the Honduran team in San Salvador on June 15, 1969, many of the Honduran spectators were set upon and mauled by the crowd. The immediate reaction in Honduras was to step up the expulsion of Salvadorean campesinos. INA documents, for example, describe the "recuperation" of more than 2,000 hectares of national and ejidal lands in three departments alone in late

---

* The Honduran position is summarized in a position paper dated March 20, 1969, presented to a meeting of the Central American Economic Council (reproduced in Carías & Slutzky 1971: 111–22).

June (report of the Departamento Jurídico in INA 1969). In response to what the newspaper *El Cronista* described as a "mass exodus" of expelled families (June 24, 1969), El Salvador closed its borders, hoping to force the Honduran government to relocate these families. When this proved of no avail, El Salvador sent its troops over the border to "defend the human rights of their countrymen" and put an end to what it termed Honduran "genocide." The attack began the Soccer War.

This sequence of events confirms at the national level two conclusions of the Langue study regarding the dynamics of land scarcity in Honduras. First, competition for Honduran farmland in the 1950's and 1960's cannot be described as a simple density-dependent process. On the one hand, the increasing concentration of arable lands (including both national and ejidal territory) in large estates was clearly a response to economic conditions and not to increasing numbers of hacendados. On the other hand, the supply of land to peasant families was small and decreasing largely because of the competitive exclusion and further encroachment by the large landowners. Rural population growth almost certainly contributed to their problems of resource scarcity as in the combination model of Chapter One. However, as R. A. White argues (1972: 820), "One must not lose sight that the basis of the [agrarian] conflicts has been and is land tenure." These conflicts were a response to relative rather than absolute resource scarcity.

Second, there is no evidence that the expulsion of Salvadoreans was the product of competitive interactions among Salvadorean and Honduran peasants. On the contrary, as FENAGH correctly perceived, Salvadorean peasants often joined forces with Honduran peasants in recuperating or occupying hacienda lands. They were not a distinct third party in the competition for land in Honduras, but participants in a two-way struggle that was already in progress before many of them arrived. In a very direct manner, they exacerbated an internal threat to the landholdings of the hacendados and increased the pressure for agrarian reform in Honduras. To the large landowners, they then became a convenient scapegoat. Their expulsion offered a means of reducing the threat of land occupations and agrarian reform.

My interpretation here coincides with the view of Alonso and Slutzky that the issue of the immigrants was a contrived one:

On the one hand, they [FENAGH] pressured for the removal of Salvadorean campesinos so that the land they occupied could be used for agrarian reform, avoiding the invasions of the landowners' private property; presenting the conflict in terms of nationality, they obtained a polarization of public opinion in favor of their interests. On the other hand, the emphasis placed on the Salvadorean invaders permitted the redefinition of the agrarian conflicts: it was then a question not of land redistribution in favor of peasants and agricultural workers, but rather of removing a minority of foreign nationals that had usurped public lands and of redistributing these lands among Hondurans. (1971: 295)

In short, FENAGH succeeded in translating an internal problem of resource competition into an external one. Its pressure on the INA to enforce the clause of the 1962 law that allowed only Hondurans to participate in the new land settlement projects was therefore an important, direct cause of the Soccer War.

Trends Since the War

What has been called "the most serious armed conflict between Latin American States in more than thirty years" (Blutstein et al. 1971: 117) lasted only four days owing to the quick intervention of the Organization of American States to arrange a cease-fire. By late July, the Salvadorean troops, which had penetrated as much as 25 miles into Honduran territory, were reluctantly withdrawn under the threat of an economic boycott by the member states of the OAS. Even now, a decade later, a more permanent settlement has yet to be achieved. The two countries have never resumed diplomatic relations, and there are only minimal exchanges of any sort between them. Border tensions continue and occasionally erupt into international incidents, as in July 1976. Honduras has effectively withdrawn from the Central American Common Market, and renewed attempts at economic integration have been thwarted by the lingering hostilities.

Events in El Salvador since the war suggest that the underlying dynamics of resource competition in that country continue to operate today. To begin with, the land tenure system remains almost completely intact, despite one abortive attempt at reform since the war. Serious talk of such a reform dates to the very "victory speech" at the end of the war by El Salvador's President at the time, Colonel Fidel Sánchez Hernández. As if to acknowledge the role of land concentration in the conflict, the speech called for public discussion of land reform and laid the groundwork for the First National Congress of Agrarian Reform, held in 1970 by the Legislative Assembly (see El Salvador, Asamblea Legislativa 1970). Nevertheless, official action was delayed until 1975 when the assembly created the Salvadorean Institute of Agrarian Transformation (ISTA). This institute was established to carry out a modest program of agrarian reforms (called "Transformations" for political reasons), as promised by President Arturo Armando Molina in his inaugural address of 1972. A second decree was issued on June 29, 1976, creating the First Project of Agrarian Transformation, a program that proposed the redistribution of some 59,000 hectares in a cotton-growing region selected for this purpose by a team of OAS experts (OAS 1974).

The region chosen for the Transformation showed the characteristic skewness of land tenure in El Salvador. Fifty-eight percent of the 3,500 farms there were under three hectares in size and accounted for only 3.3 percent of the farmland. At the other extreme, a full 60 percent of the farmland was held by a mere 2.9 percent of the farms; and more than half of this land was owned by just five landowners. The project, as announced, stipulated new ownership limits, putting the maximum holding at 35.0 hectares and the minimum at 3.0. It also provided for the purchase of any holdings in excess of the limit from their present owners at market prices. This land was then to be distributed to some 12,000 peasant families (Burke 1976; Colindres 1976).

The announcement of the project stirred immediate controversy in El Salvador. An acrimonious debate in the media between the military government and the National Association of Private Enterprise (ANEP) began within ten days of the announcement and continued for several months (this debate is revewed in Zamora 1976 and Martín-Baró 1977). Meanwhile, the large landowners from the project area and allies from other areas quickly formed a protest group called FARO (the Agricultural Front of the Oriental Region), whose acronym means "guiding light." This group denounced the project in a series of manifestos that "abounded in personal attacks, veiled threats, distorted imputations, and even obvious calumnies" (Martín-Baró 1977: 7). On October 19, after three months of heated debate, members of the Legislative Assembly bowed to the pressure, and so stiffly amended the project as to annul it. To date, no action has been taken to "transform" any lands at all in the country.

The abandonment of this project, together with the fraudulent national election of President Carlos Humberto Romero in February 1977, helps explain the increasing wave of political kidnappings, assassinations, and popular demonstrations in El Salvador in the last few years. Among those slain have been Foreign Minister Mauricio Borgonovo Pohl, several Jesuit priests, the Rector of the National University, and a former Speaker of the National Legislature, many of whom publicly supported the Transformation project (for details see U.S. House of Representatives 1977).

The killing of the Jesuits, moreover, was a response of the right-wing organization known as the White Warriors Union to the clergy's increasing support of emerging peasant organizations, particularly the Union of Agricultural Workers (UTC) and the Christian Federation of Campesinos (FECCAS). In the years since the Soccer War, these organizations have played an important role in the growing numbers of land invasions in rural areas. One such invasion in the municipality of San Pedro Perulapán was violently repressed in March 1978 by the combined action of the Salvadorean armed forces and a rural right-wing paramilitary group called ORDEN (National Democratic Organization). Members of the UTC and FECCAS fled to neighboring municipalities, including Tenancingo, where they were again confronted by army tanks and armed members of ORDEN. The incident, described in detail in a report from the office of the Archbishop of San Salvador (Secretaria de Comunicación Social del Arzobispado de San Salvador 1978), dramatically emphasizes the land problems that continue to confront the rural poor of El Salvador.

Knowledgable observers and former government officials feel strongly that the country, having forfeited the chance for a peaceful "Agrarian Transformation," is now on the verge of a major popular uprising. Competitive exclusion continues, and the population is still growing at a rate of more than 3.5 percent a year.

In Honduras, the National Agrarian Institute continues to find itself caught in the middle, with both the large landholders of FENAGH and the peasant organizations ANACH and UNC bringing powerful pressure to bear on every plan for agrarian reform. Campesino land occupations have occurred intermittently since 1969 (see

R. A. White 1977: 175ff). Throughout 1970 and into 1971, the INA responded favorably to the occupations of public lands and assisted the campesinos in establishing more than 70 production cooperatives. ANACH and UNC, which handled the land petitions from local peasant groups, grew rapidly in both size and influence. But with the election of President Ramón Ernesto Cruz from the conservative National Party in 1971, FENAGH succeeded in getting Sandoval removed from office. Without his direction, the INA's reform projects lost much of their momentum.

The campesino federations regained their influence when, with their support, the conservative regime was toppled in a bloodless military coup in 1972. The government of President Oswaldo López Arellano quickly issued Interim Decree No. 8, enabling INA to force landowners to rent under-utilized portions of their holdings. In the next two years, more than 500 peasant settlements were established, largely on lands belonging to private estates (K. H. Parsons 1976: 18).

Meanwhile, in 1973, the campesino organizations launched a campaign for a revised agrarian reform law that would provide for the permanent expropriation of under-utilized lands on private estates. The campaign gained momentum when Hurricane Fifi ravaged the north coast in 1974, destroying an estimated 60 percent of the country's agricultural production and intensifying the plight of the rural poor. After long debate, a new agrarian reform law, No. 170, was enacted in January 1975. The law called for some 600,000 hectares of land to be redistributed among 120,000 families over a five-year period. It set regional limits on the size of landholdings (in every case below 500 hectares) and specified that owners would be paid in agrarian bonds for their lands affected by the INA. A stated purpose of the law was to replace the traditional minifundia and latifundia with modern, cooperative peasant enterprises (Programa de Capacitación Campesina para la Reforma Agraria 1975: 101).

Predictably, the promulgation of Law 170 drew opposition from FENAGH, as well as the Honduran Council of Private Business (COHEP). The head of FENAGH, for example, charged that the land reform law "attacks private property, the democratic system, liberty and individuality" (*Latin America*, April 11, 1975: 106). As opposition to the law grew among these groups, a scandal involving a $1,250,000 bribe from the United Brands Company forced President López

Arellano to resign. Implementation of Law 170 was delayed, causing the campesino groups to mobilize again in protest.

On May 19, 1975, the UNC sponsored the invasion of nearly 120 haciendas in ten departments. Threats of forcible removal by the authorities prompted the campesinos to withdraw soon thereafter from lands they had occupied, but tensions remained high. In June of that year, a local military commander in Olancho sided with the landowners in organizing an armed attack on a UNC training headquarters. Five peasant leaders were killed in the assault; nine additional bodies were found later on the estate of one of Olancho's wealthiest landowners (*Latin America*, July 18, 1975: 220). The Olancho murders stimulated further protest by campesino groups, which formed a united front with a total membership of over 150,000. In October the front issued an ultimatum, threatening more land invasions if the redistribution of land under the new law was further delayed.

In an apparent victory for the campesino groups, the new president, Colonel Juan Alberto Melgar Castro, decided to reappoint Sandoval Corea to head the INA. Yet throughout 1976 and early 1977, the efforts of INA officials to implement Law 170 were undermined by continued denunciations on the part of FENAGH, COHEP, and other organizations representing the interests of large landowners. Opposition slowed the momentum of the reform to the point where, on March 15, 1977, Sandoval Corea resigned—an action that many observers believe marks the end of the reform policy initiated in 1972. The UNC responded to this development by staging a new wave of land invasions, reminiscent of actions in El Salvador since the ISTA debacle. Even now, a full decade after the Soccer War, it is clear that the struggle between the peasants and the large landowners of Honduras is far from resolved.

Conclusions and Implications

Events both before and after the Soccer War lend support to three major conclusions of this study. First, they plainly show that in both El Salvador and Honduras, competition for land is not a simple, density-dependent process. Indeed, evidence in each case suggests that competition does not occur so much among peasants as between peasants and large landowners. In El Salvador, the rural poor continue to be excluded from more than 60 percent of the nation's flattest and most fertile land. Recent attempts to start an Agrarian Transformation met stiff resistance and failed to reverse the distributional dynamics that have reduced the land base of the poor almost twice as much in recent history as their increased numbers. In Honduras, similarly, access to land has been sharply affected by competition between large landowners and small farmers. Particularly since World War II, the growing demand for land by the large commercial farmers has often meant a reduction in the lands available to campesinos. Beginning in 1962, some attempt has been made to restructure the land distribution, but the reform has been unable to equalize major disparities due to the resistance of powerful landed interests. In both countries population growth contributes to and intensifies the scarcity of resources—but it cannot be said to determine them. These examples conform most closely to the combination model of Chapter One.

Second, the conflict between El Salvador and Honduras may be seen as a product of these dynamics of competition within each of those countries. On the one hand, our analysis has shown that competitive exclusion in El Salvador forced an increasing number of landless and land-poor peasants to migrate to Honduras in search of land to farm. Indeed, we have seen that a close correlation exists between the life-and-death consequences of land scarcity and the tendency of the rural poor to leave an area permanently. On the other hand, our evidence indicates that the Salvadorean migration then exacerbated the process of resource competition between large and small farmers in Honduras. Pressure from the large landowners, the group most affected by the Salvadorean influx, resulted in the expulsion of the immigrants and converted what had been competition within the countries into competition between them. Given that distributional dynamics played a key role both in the emigration of Salvadoreans to Honduras and in their expulsion, we must conclude that the Soccer War cannot accurately be described as a population problem.

Third, it seems clear from the subsequent developments in El Salvador and Honduras that the Soccer War had very different effects on the process of resource competition in the two countries. In El Salvador, the war caused the return of some 130,000 emigrants, who then joined the ranks of the country's landless and unemployed or underemployed. Today, though pressures for land reforms are greater than ever, a small group of large landholders is still able to prevent even a modest agricultural transformation. In Honduras, by contrast, the effect was to reinforce a process of land reform that started with the help of—and, one might say, in part because of—the Salvadorean immigrants. Their presence contributed to the mobilization of Honduran peasants into local defense groups and eventually into national peasant federations. Thanks to the activities of these organizations, Honduras in 1975 appeared to be "the only Central American country where campesinos play a decisive role in the process of agrarian reform" (Santos de Morais 1975: 16). It remains to be seen if this momentum, spurred by the Soccer War, will outlast recent political changes.

This analysis, in conclusion, underscores the need for human ecologists to extend models of resource competition to include a distributional component. Although density-dependent formulations may be adequate for largely asocial animal populations, there are two major reasons why distributional dynamics must be taken into account if we are to understand human resource competition. First, the distribution of resources within a population need not be a fixed parameter. As we have seen in both El Salvador and Honduras, there have been major distributional changes within the recent past. Moreover, these changes have been at least as consequential as population growth. In ecological analyses of resource scarcity, distribution can therefore be a variable of primary importance.

Second, distribution—particularly in the case of land—can introduce a non-physical component of structure to the habitat. As suggested by this study, competitive exclusion can lead to the concentration of inhabitants in a given area. When this occurs, it is scientifically unsound to attribute the consequences of high density (e.g., environmental degradation, out-migration) to population growth. The existence of such crowded communities may be the result of distributional dynamics on a broader scale.

These considerations suggest the need for a re-evaluation of evidence linking other international conflicts with population pressure (on this point, see Williams 1971; Choucri 1974). Although this association has long been asserted in the literature (e.g., Hankins 1940; Russell 1964; Ehrlich & Ehrlich 1972), it assumes that a process of "generalized competition" is of overriding influence. Because human societies, particularly those we call nation-states, are far from atomistic assemblages of individuals, *a priori* grounds for this assumption are weak at best. Moreover, as we have seen, this assumption is invalid for the Soccer War, a case held by some to be the best example of density-dependent processes. Even in the most densely populated mainland country in this hemisphere, competition is socially organized in a way that has significant distributional consequences. To ignore the dynamics of distribution (as has been suggested by Ehrlich & Ehrlich 1976, for example) is thus to ignore what may often be a major, if not the major, cause of resource scarcity.

Reutlinger and Selowsky, in their recent study of malnutrition and poverty (1976), have reached a similar conclusion. Their calculations of calorie consumption by family income suggest that in most countries around the world the problem of malnutrition is a problem of internal distribution. Aggregate supply-demand comparisons lead to a gross underestimate of the severity of the problem and to false conclusions about its solution. As the authors suggest, malnutrition would still be prevalent even if aggregate deficits were alleviated. Their analysis reinforces the findings of Valverde et al. 1977 and Rawson & Valverde 1976 discussed in Chapter Two. If we may assume that an inverse relationship exists between nutritional status and child mortality, their log-linear regression model is also consistent with my own findings.

To focus on aggregate data and average abundance is also to ignore an important amount of variability in the consequences of resource scarcity. For example, the rates of out-migration from families of a rural community in El Salvador have here been shown to vary generally as an inverse function of their access to land. Moreover, nearly three-quarters of all the out-migrants came from families with less than the average landholding. Even at the local level, then, land distribution is an important factor in rural out-migration. At the national level, one would expect to find a similar trend. R. Paul Shaw's study "Land Tenure and The Rural Exodus" (1976) confirms this expectation for other Latin American countries. In the case of Peru, for example, Shaw relates departmental rates of rural male emigration from 1940 to 1961 with both an aggregate measure of density (total rural agricultural population divided by total arable land) and a measure of density corrected for land concentration (total rural agricultural population divided by the total arable land excluding latifundias of 500 or more hectares). The adjusted R^2 values increase from 0.04 to 0.44, respectively (p. 87). Results such as these confirm that aggregate density measures are not adequate for understanding migration as a response to resource scarcity.

As I have shown, aggregate measures are also inadequate for the analysis of child mortality patterns. The use of aggregate data for El Salvador's rural child mortality rates not only would conceal a two- to threefold differential associated with variation in peasant family land-holdings, but would also complicate and confound the analysis of the cause. The argument that more medicine and better sanitation are necessary to reduce the country's rural mortality, for example, ignores the fact that the people who most need these improvements are also the people who can least afford them. As long as land continues to grow increasingly scarce for El Salvador's small farmers, there is little hope that the mortality differentials documented here will disappear.

Some of the recent research on fertility trends in less-developed countries likewise attests to the importance of distributional factors in resource scarcity. William Rich (1973) and James Kocher (1973), for example, have found that the average income of the poorest 60 percent of the populations in their sample countries correlates much more closely (and negatively) with fertility trends than does the average income of the population as a whole. One possible reason for this, Rich suggests (1973: 13), is that the assurance of high rates of survival provides an important motivation for small families (see also May & Heer 1968; Lipton 1977). The data I collected in Tenancingo are wholly consistent with this hypothesis. So, too, is information from Kerala, India, described in Ratcliffe 1978. There, in contrast to other Indian states, "Widespread political participation has resulted in a more equitable distribution of land, income, and services, including education" (p. 139). Associated with these recent changes, mortality and then fertility levels in Kerala have dropped in comparison with India as a whole. The examples are few and far between, but the implications are highly significant: it may well be that distributional factors are a major influence on population growth itself.

Appendix

Mathematical Models
of Resource Competition

The most widely used mathematical model of intraspecific resource competition was first proposed by Verhulst in 1838. Also called the "logistic equation," the model assumes that the per-capita growth rate of a given population (dN/Ndt) decreases in a simple linear fashion with population size (N):

$$\frac{dN}{Ndt} = a - bN$$

The constants a and b in this expression are sometimes rewritten as r and r/K respectively, where r is then called the population's "intrinsic rate of natural increase," and K is defined as the "carrying capacity" for the population in a given environment. The equation can then be written

$$\frac{dN}{Ndt} = r\left(1 - \frac{N}{K}\right)$$

In this simple model, each individual of N can be thought of as reducing the availability of some essential resource by an amount equal to $1/K$. The term $(1 - N/K)$ thus represents the effect of density-dependent resource competition on the average ability of individuals to survive and reproduce as measured by dN/Ndt.

The logistic model was extended to allow for two competing populations by Lotka in 1925. Lotka's model assumes that the per-capita growth rate of one population (dN_1/N_1dt) is a decreasing linear function not only of its own population size (N_1) but also of the size of the competing population (N_2). Thus,

$$\frac{dN_1}{dt} = r_1N_1\left(\frac{K_1 - N_1 - \alpha N_2}{K_1}\right),$$

where r_1 and K_1 are defined for N_1 as above and where α is a constant "competition coefficient" equivalent to the per-capita harm to N_1 caused by N_2. If it is likewise assumed that N_1 has harmful effects on N_2 in proportion to its numbers, an equivalent expression for the growth rate of N_2 can be expressed as follows:

$$\frac{dN_2}{dt} = r_2 N_2 \left(\frac{K_2 - N_2 - \beta N_1}{K_2} \right)$$

In these expressions, the competing populations are assumed to have density-dependent inhibiting effects on each other's survival and/or reproduction. At equilibrium (when $dN_1/dt = 0$ and $dN_2/dt = 0$), these equations can be used to show which parameter values permit the two populations to coexist or permit one population to outcompete and replace the other (e.g., Wilson & Bossert 1971). The equations have been generalized to "i" populations and tested with some success using laboratory populations of protozoans (see, e.g., Vandermeer 1969).

In this simple model, each individual of N_2 can be thought of as reducing the availability of some essential resource to N_1 by an amount α/K_1 (and vice versa, β/K_2). Each individual in N_1 also reduces the total available resource (K_1) by an amount equal to $1/K_1$ (hence the term $(K_1 - N_1)/K_1$). Both intra- and interpopulational competition are therefore assumed by the model to be simple density-dependent processes.

As shown in Figure 1.2 and described in Chapter One, this is really only one of at least three possible models of resource competition among organisms with some semblance of social structure, including human beings. The distinction between the alternative models can be summarized in a mathematical fashion as follows. For simplicity, the discussion is restricted to competitive dynamics within a single population.

In density-dependent Malthusian models, per-capita resource availability (R_c) is assumed to be a simple function of the total resource supply (R) and the size of the consumer population (N):

$$R_c = R/N$$

If we further assume that changes through time in the total stock of the resource are negligible (i.e., $\Delta R/\Delta t = 0$, as may be reasonable in the case of land resources, for example), then the competitive effects of population growth over a short interval Δt will cause a change in per-capita resource availability, expressed as:

$$\Delta R_c/\Delta t = (-R/N^2)(\Delta N/\Delta t)$$

where $\Delta N/\Delta t$ represents population growth over the same interval. One implication of this expression deserves special mention—the effects of population growth on per-capita resource availability under these assumptions will actually tend to diminish as the population, hence N^2, grows large. Neo-Malthusian theorists have generally ignored this deduction that follows from their assumptions.

For simplicity in the distributional model, assume that there are only two subpopulations, N_p and N_w (each internally conforming to the assumptions of Figure 1.2A) competing between them for differential access to R. If we further assume for the sake of argument that the N_p and N_w remain constant through time, then per-capita resource availability (R_{cp}) for the poorer sub-population, N_p, will be a function of R, N_p, and the resource monopolized by the wealthier subpopulation, R_w:

$$R_{cp} = (R - R_w)/N_p$$

This means that $\Delta R_{cp}/\Delta t = 1/N_p[\Delta R/\Delta t - \Delta R_w/\Delta t]$. Letting $\Delta R/\Delta t = 0$ again,

$$\Delta R_{cp}/\Delta t = -1/N_p(\Delta R_w/\Delta t)$$

where $1/N_p$ is a constant. Change in per-capita resource availability among the poor is here a simple function of what the rich have taken.

Where both population and distribution may change in time, as in the combination model, competitive losses in resource availability within the sub-group N_p may be determined as follows:

$$R_{cp} = (R - R_w)/N_p$$

If $\Delta R/\Delta t$ again $= 0$, then

$$\Delta R_{cp}/\Delta t = -(\Delta R_w/\Delta t)1/N_p - (R_p/N_p{}^2)(\Delta N_p/\Delta t)$$

According to this equation, the effects of distributional change on per-capita resource availability among the poor may be considered negligible relative to population growth only when

$$\Delta R_w/\Delta t << (R - R_w)(\Delta N_p/N_p\Delta t)$$

The last term of this expression, $(\Delta N_p/N_p\Delta t)$, is equivalent to the per-capita rate of growth of the population over an interval Δt. For some of the world's large and rapidly growing countries, this term is approximately constant for years or even decades at a time. The term $(R - R_w)$, however, will not be constant if there is ongoing distributional change in access to resources. Where R_w is both a substantial fraction of R and growing, $(R - R_w)$ will decrease in time. The expression above therefore implies that distributional dynamics, represented by the term $\Delta R_w/\Delta t$, may well increase in relative importance through time in large and expanding populations. This implication seriously challenges a common assumption of neo-Malthusian arguments—that on-going distributional dynamics are negligible relative to population growth as a cause of resource scarcity.

Sample Survey Questionnaire

This translation amalgamates the questionnaires I used in Tenancingo and Langue. Where the questions differed, I have used the italic labels "L only" and "T only." For easier reading, I have simplified the questionnaire in several respects. Most of the answers in the "No" category, for example, were assigned separate numbers for the purpose of coding and keypunching the data; I have dropped all such answers when they did not involve a follow-up question. I have also combined many multi-part questions and dropped their numbers; amended or even omitted some of the instructions to the interviewers; and recast most of the questions to use merely "spouse" and "marry" where the interviewer would have substituted "companion" and "living together" for an acompañada relationship. I will be happy to supply the complete questionnaires, in Spanish, on request.

Good morning/afternoon. I have come to visit you as part of a study of Salvadorean/Honduran families and agriculture. It is a study organized by students from a university in North America with the assistance of Salvadorean/Honduran interviewers. The municipality of Tenancingo/Langue was chosen for the study because of its friendly and helpful people and because of our interest in the agricultural practices of this area.

The object of my visit is to ask you a few questions. May I ask that you answer all questions as accurately as you can, since each one is important for the study. *The results will be confidential and will not mention any names.* From these interviews, we will make a general descriptive summary of the community and of its needs for future years.

For this reason, we thank you for your cooperation and time in helping us. First, I would like to ask you a few questions about yourself. Please tell me:

1. When were you born (month and year)?
2. How old are you (in completed years)?
3. Where were you born (department, municipality, and hamlet)?

4a. (If born in the same hamlet where interviewed): Have you always lived in this hamlet? (If yes, go to Question 5.) (If no): Why did you leave here? Why did you come back?

4b. (If born in another hamlet or municipality): When did you come to this hamlet? Why did you come to live here?

5. Are you married (by the Church), living together (*acompañada* or *acompañado*), separated, widowed, or single? (If single, skip to Question 8.)

7a. (If married at present): How many years have you lived with your spouse?

7b. (If widowed/separated): How many years did you live with your spouse?

8. Do you know how to read and write? (If yes): How many grades did you study in school?

9. In the past year (12 months) did you undertake any activity or work that enabled you to make some money? (If yes): What did you do? (If no): Not even during the coffee or cotton harvest? (If still no, skip to Question 13.)

10. Normally, how much did you make per month in this work?

11. How many months did you work last year?

12. Do you commonly help out with work in the fields? *T only.*

[If the women we interviewed in Tenancingo were younger than 25 or older than 55, this is where the interview ended. In the Langue survey, the interviewer skipped the next set of questions and went to the sequence beginning at No. 18.]

Now I would like to ask you some questions about your family.

13. In your opinion, what is the best age for a woman to marry? *T only.*

14. How many children do you think a woman should have? (If the respondent answers "All those that God sends" or "that come along," ask): What is the best number of children for God to send/to come along? *T only.*

15. At what age is it best for a son to begin helping with work in the fields? To begin working for an income? Living apart from his family? *T only.*

16. At what age is it best for a daughter to begin helping in the household? Working for an income? Living apart from her family? *T only.*

17. What do you think is the best inheritance one can leave to one's children? *T only.*

Turning now to your spouse: (If single, skip to No. 28.)

18. What is his/her name?

19. Where was he/she born (department, municipality, and hamlet)?

20. When was he/she born (month and year)?

21. How old is he/she (in completed years)? (If deceased): How many years ago did he/she die? How old was he/she then?

22. How old was he/she when he/she became your spouse?

23. Does he/she know how to read and write? (If yes): How many grades did he/she study in school?

24. Does your husband work in agriculture? (If yes): How many days a week in general? *T only.*

25. Did he ever live in the country of Honduras? (If no, skip to No. 26.) (If yes): Where did he live (department, municipality, and hamlet)? In what year did he go off to Honduras? Why did he go there? Did you go with him? In what year did he return to El Salvador? Did he have land in Honduras? (If so): Approximately how much? *T only.*

26. How many families from this hamlet left for Honduras before the (1969) war? *T only.*

27. In the last 12 months, did your spouse have some other activity or work that enabled him/her to make some money? (If yes): What does he/she do? Of the last 12 months, how many did he/she work at this other occupation? Normally, how much did he/she make in this work per month? (If no): He/she made no money last year?

28. In general, how much income does your family make in a month, including what your spouse and children contribute? (If the respondent cannot specify): Of the following amounts, tell me which is closest to the amount your family earns in a month (in *colones/lempiras*): 0, 1–10, 10–20, 20–30, 30–40, 40–50, 50–60, 60–70, 70–80, 80–90, 90–100, 100–125, 125–150, 150–200, 200–300, 300–400, 400–500, 500–600, more than 600.

Now let's talk about agriculture. [In Tenancingo, the interviewer now jumped to No. 37.]

29. What crops are you planning to grow this year? *L only.*

30. Normally, do you burn your plots each year before planting? (If yes): Why do you burn them? What does the burning do? (If no): Why don't you burn them? *L only.*

31. Do you burn pastureland? (If yes): Why? (If respondent has pastureland and answers no): Why don't you burn it? *L only.*

32. Do you have any parcel of plowable land (*tierra arada*)? (If yes): For how many consecutive years do you cultivate this plowable land without leaving it fallow? Does this include using fertilizer of any kind? *L only.*

33. Do you have any parcel of *tierra a bordón* (uneven land requiring the use of a planting stick)? (If no, jump to No. 35.). For how many consecutive years to do cultivate this land without leaving it fallow? Does this include using fertilizer of any kind?

34a. Speaking of *tierra a bordón*, how do you use a parcel of this land in the first planting in the first year following a fallow period? In the second planting? *L only.*

34b. How do you use it in the first planting in the second year following a fallow period? In the second planting? (Continue until the respondent says fallow again.) *L only.*

35a. How do you decide when it is time to let a parcel lie fallow? What indications tell you it is time? *L only.*

35b. After a period of continuous use, how long do you normally allow your land to remain fallow? *L only.*

35c. How long would the fallow period be ideally? *L only.*

35d. Why do you let your land lie fallow? *L only.*

36. If we were to plant maize in a manzana of land like yours for its first year after fallow, how much would we harvest in the first year under normal conditions? In the second year? (Continue until respondent says fallow again.) *L only.*

37. How many parcels or plots of land are you using this year? How many of these are your own? How many belong to others?

Please describe to me the plots you are using one by one, beginning with the largest. (Repeat all parts of Question 38 for each plot.)

38a. In what hamlet is it located?

38b. What size is it? (specify units)

38c. Is it plowable land or land requiring a planting stick?

38d. Is it ejidal land (*L only*)? Rented land? Property? Your own or some relative's? Other (specify)?

38e. How did you obtain this land?

38f. How many years have you used it?

38g. This year, how are you using it? How much is in crops? Which crops and how much of each? How much is in pasture? How much in fallow? How much in unused woodlands?

[Items 38h– 38j, omitted here, repeat Question 38g for each of the three previous years.]

39. Therefore, you have *x* plots of land in all, of which *x* are ejidal (*L only*), *x* are rented, *x* are property, and *x* are other (specify). Is that correct? (If respondent disagrees, review the responses to Question 38 with him/her and make corrections before continuing.)

40. In addition, last year *x* amount was dedicated to crops, *x* to pasture, *x* to fallow, and *x* to unused woodland. Is this correct? (Again, correct any discrepancies.)

41. Do you work this land by yourself or does someone help you? (If helped): By children? How many children help you? By spouse? By salaried workers? By others (specify)? *L only.*

42. How much land did you have in all last year? Two years ago? Five years ago? Ten years ago?

43. (If not single): How much land did you have when you were married?

44. What is the greatest quantity of land you have ever had? (If more than present total): Why do you have less now? (If less than present total): How did you obtain more?

45. At this time, how many head of cattle do you have? How many pigs? Goats? Poultry? *L only.*

46. Did you sell any animals in the last year? (If yes): What animals? What did you earn in total from the sale of these animals? (If no): All animals went for family consumption? *L only.*

47. Did you sell some part of your harvest last year? (If yes): What sort of crops? How much did you earn last year through the sale of these crops? (If no): All of the harvest was consumed by the family?

Now I would like to ask you to tell me something about your mother.

48. Is your mother living? (If deceased): How long ago did she die?

49. How old is she/was she when she died?

50. Where does/did she live (department, municipality, and hamlet)? *T only.*

51. Where was she born (department, municipality, and hamlet)? *T only.*

52. And your father, is he alive? (If deceased): How long ago did he die?

53. How old is he/was he when he died?

54. Where does/did he live (department, municipality, and hamlet)? *L only.*
55. Where was he born (department, municipality, and hamlet)? *L only.*
56. What does/did your father do for a living?
57. When you were young, how much land did your parents use?
58. How much of this land was property of the family?
59. How much land does your father use now/did he use before his death?
60. Did you inherit any land from your parents? (If yes): How much land did you receive? From whom? (If no): What happened to your parents' land?

Now I would like to ask about your brothers and sisters.
61. How many children did your mother have in all, including any who lived even a very short time?
62. Were there any who died young, before becoming adults? (If yes): How many?
63. How many living brothers and sisters do you have? (Check Questions 61–63 for consistency.)
64. Are you the oldest of these children? (If no): What number child are you?

Let's begin with the oldest of your brothers and sisters. (Repeat all parts of Question 65 for each brother and sister.) *T only.*
65a. What is his/her name? *T only.*
65b. Male or female? *T only.*
65c. Is he/she alive? (If yes): How old is he/she? (If no): How long ago did he/she die? How old was he/she then?
65d. Where does he/she live now/where did he/she live before death?
65e. Where was he/she born?
65f. Is/was he/she married, living together, separated, widowed, or single? *T only.*
65g. Does/did he/she have children? How many?
65h. What is the age of his/her oldest child? of the youngest? *T only.*
65i. How old is his/her spouse? (If deceased): How long ago did the spouse die? At what age? *T only.*
65j. Does the family of this brother/sister depend on agriculture for their living?
65k. How much land does his/her family use? *T only.*
65l. Did he/she receive part of this land as an inheritance from your parents? How much? *T only.*
[If respondent is single and has no children, jump to No. 85/86 below.]
66. Is your mother-in-law living at the present time? (If deceased): How long ago did she die? *T only.*
67. How old is she/was she when she died? *T only.*
68. Where does/did she live (department, municipality, and hamlet)? *T only.*
69. Including your husband, how many surviving children did your mother-in-law have? *T only.*

70. Is your father-in-law living at present? (If deceased): How long ago did he die? *T only.*

71. How old is he/was he when he died? *T only.*

72. Does/did your father-in-law work in agriculture? *T only.*

73. How much land did your in-laws use when your spouse lived with them? *T only.*

74. How much of this was family property? *T only.*

75. Did your spouse inherit any land from his/her family? (If yes): How much? From whom? (If no): What happened to the family's land?

Finally, let's talk about your own family.

76. How many living children do you have?

77. How many of your children have died? (If none, go to Question 78.) (If more than one, repeat 77a–77e for each child.)

77a. The first/next of these children to die was male or female?

77b. When was the child born?

77c. When did the child die?

77d. How old was the child?

77e. What caused the child's death?

Now let's talk about your living children, beginning with the oldest. (Repeat the series for each living child, including any who do not live with the family.)

78a. What is the child's name? *T only.*

78b. Male or female? *T only.*

78c. In what year was he/she born? *T only.*

78d. Where was the child born? Where were you living at the time (department, municipality, and hamlet)? *T only.*

78e. How old is this child?

78f. Does he/she live with you at this time? (If no): Where does he/she live (department, municipality, and canton)? When did he/she go there? Why did he/she leave? *T only.*

78g. Is this son/daughter married, living together, separated, widowed, or single? *T only.*

78h. At what age did he/she marry? *T only.*

78i. Does this child help with family agriculture? With household chores? (If yes): At what age did he/she begin helping?

78j. Did this son/daughter have any work that enabled him/her to make some money this past year? (If yes): What did he/she do? (If no, skip 78k–78m and go on to next child.)

78k. How much did he/she make in a month normally?

78l. Did he/she contribute some of this to the family? (If yes): How much per month?

78m. At what age did this child begin to work for an income?

79. Do all your children have the same father/mother? (Check response in Tenancingo against last names.)

80. Thus, you have had x children in all, of whom x are living. Is that correct? Of these, x help with the family income. Is that also correct? *T only.*

81. (For each child between 10 and 15 years of age): What occupation would you prefer this child to have as an adult? *T only*.

82. How many more children would you like to have? Why/why not? *T only*.

83. What do you think you will give your children as an inheritance? (If land, note the quantity for each child.)

We have almost finished. However, I did want to ask you out of curiosity (*L only*):

84. Were there any Salvadorean families living in this hamlet before the conflict with El Salvador? (If yes): How many families were there? Did they also work in agriculture? How much land did each of these families use? How did they obtain that land? How were your relations with these families? When and how did they leave this area? (If no): There were no Salvadorean families in this hamlet?

And finally, as my last question:

85. In your opinion, what is the most serious agricultural problem in this area? *L only*.

86. To what do you attribute the scarcity of land here? *T only*.

Post-interview Items

87. Others present during the interview: spouse, mother or father, adult male, adult female, children, infant, no one.

88. Type of house: palm-thatched hut, wattle-and-daub with tile roof, adobe with tile roof, cinder-block.

89. Interview was obtained on: first visit, second visit, other (specify).

90. House number (from map).

91. Location (hamlet and locality).

92. Income verification and check on Question 28:

Respondent earns	——— per month
Spouse earns	——— per month
Children earn	——— per month
Sale of animals ($\div$ 12)	———
Sale of crops ($\div$ 12)	———
Total monthly income	———

(If the total is off by more than one category from the answer given to Question 28, review the figures given there with the respondent.)

Bibliography

Bibliography

I have used the following abbreviations in the text citations:

CELADE	Centro Latinoamericano de Demografía
CEPAL	Comisión Económica Para América Latina
CONAPLAN	Consejo Nacional de Planificación
CONSUPLAN	Consejo Superior de Planificación Económica
ECLA	Economic Commission on Latin America
ESDGEC	El Salvador, Dirección General de Estadística y Censos
ESMAG	El Salvador, Ministerior de Agricultura y Ganadería
HDGEC	Honduras, Dirección General de Estadística y Censos
IGN	Instituto Geográfico Nacional
IIES	Instituto de Investigaciones Económicas y Sociales
INA	Instituto Nacional Agrario
INCAP	Instituto de Nutrición de Centro América y Panama
OAS	Organization of American States

Adams, R. N. 1967. Nationalization. In *Handbook of Middle American Indians*, pp. 469–89. Austin, Tex.

Aguilar Girón, R. 1967. *Estudio económico Agrícola del cultivo de algodón, ciclo 1966–67*. San Salvador.

Alonso, E., and D. Slutzky. 1971. La estructura agraria de El Salvador y Honduras: Sus consecuencias sociales y el conflicto actual. In Carías and Slutzky, cited below, pp. 243–97.

Anderson, T. P. 1971. *Matanza: El Salvador's Communist Revolt of 1932*. Lincoln, Neb.

Annegers, J. F. 1967. Agricultural resources and food supply in El Salvador. M. A. thesis, Geography Department, Michigan State University.

Anuario estadístico. 1911–23, 1927–75. El Salvador, Dirección General de Estadística y Censos. San Salvador. (For respective years.)

Asociación Cafetalera de El Salvador. 1940. *Primer censo nacional de café*. San Salvador.

Asociación Demográfica Salvadoreña. 1974. *Encuesta nacional de fecundidad*. San Salvador.

Ayala Kreutz, R. S. 1968. El crecimiento de la población y producción de alimentos en El Salvador: 1950, 1965 y 1980. Thesis, Facultad de Ciencias Agronómicas, Universidad de El Salvador.

Bachmura, F. T. 1971. Toward economic reconciliation in Central America. *World Affairs* 133 (4): 283–92.

Bahr, H. M. 1972. Values and population policy. In. Bahr et al., cited below, pp. 267–99.

Bahr, H. M., et al., eds. 1972. *Population, Resources, and the Future: Non-Malthusian Perspectives*. Provo, Utah.

Barberena, S. I. 1892. *Descripción geográfica y estadística de la República de El Salvador*. San Salvador.

Barberena, S. I., and P. S. Fonseca. 1909–14. *Monografías departamentales*. San Salvador.

Barlett, P. F. 1975. Agricultural change in Paso: The structure of decision making in a Costa Rican peasant community. Ph.D. dissertation, Columbia University.

———. 1976. Labor efficiency and the mechanism of agricultural evolution. *Journal of Anthropological Research* 32: 124–40.

———. 1977. The structure of decision making in Paso. *American Ethnologist* 4 (2): 285–307.

Barón Castro, R. 1978 (1942). *La población de El Salvador*. San Salvador.

Beresford, J. 1970. Cotton saved by strict programme. *The Financial Times*, April 27: 31.

Birch, L. C. 1957. The meanings of competition. *American Naturalist* 91: 5–18.

Blutstein, H. I., et al. 1971. *Area Handbook for Honduras*. Washington, D.C.

Bodley, J. H. 1976. *Anthropology and Contemporary Human Problems*. Menlo Park, Calif.

Borgstrom, G. 1973. *The Food and People Dilemma*. North Scituate, Mass.

Boserup, E. 1965. *The Conditions of Agricultural Growth: The Economics of Agrarian Change Under Population Pressure*. Chicago.

Bourne, C., et al. 1947. *Preliminary Survey of Conservation Possibilities in El Salvador*. San Salvador.

Brand, C. A. 1972. The background of capitalistic underdevelopment: Honduras to 1913. Ph.D. dissertation, University of Pittsburgh.

Brannon, M. P. 1934. *La investigación estadística: Origen, desarollo y estado actual de la investigación estadística de El Salvador*. San Salvador.

Brockelman, W. Y. 1969. An analysis of density effects and predation in *Bufo americanus* tadpoles. *Ecology* 50: 632–44.

Browning, D. 1971. *El Salvador: Landscape and Society*. Oxford, Eng.

Browning, H. L. 1970. Some sociological considerations of population pressure on resources. In Zelinsky et al., pp. 71–82.

Brunn, S., and P. Thomas. 1972. Socio-economic environments and internal migration: The case of Tegucigalpa, Honduras. *Social and Economic Studies* 4: 463–73.

————. 1973. The migration system of Tegucigalpa, Honduras. In R. N. Thomas, ed., *Population Dynamics of Latin America*, pp. 63–82. East Lansing, Mich.

Burke, M. 1976. El sistema de plantación y la proletarización del trabajo agrícola en El Salvador. *Estudios Centroamericanos* 31 (335/36): 473–86.

Cable, V. 1969. The "football" war and the Central American Common Market. *International Affairs* (London) 45: 658–71.

Cancian, F. 1965. *Economics and Prestige in a Maya Community*. Stanford, Calif.

Capa, C., and J. M. Stycos. 1974. *Margin of Life: Population and Poverty in the Americas*. New York.

Cardona Lazo, A. 1939. *Monografías departamentales*. San Salvador.

Cardoso, C. F. S. 1973. La formación de la hacienda cafetalera en Costa Rica (Siglo XIX). *Estudios Sociales Centroamericanos* 6: 22–50.

————. 1975. Historia económica del café en Centroamérica. *Estudios Sociales Centroamericanos* 10: 9–55.

Carías, M. V., and D. Slutzky, eds. 1971. *La guerra inútil: Análisis socioeconómico del conflicto entre Honduras y El Salvador*. San José, Costa Rica.

Centro Latinoamericano de Demografía. 1974. *Boletín demográfico* 7: 13.

Chamberlain, R. S. 1967. *The Conquest and Colonization of Honduras, 1502–1550*. New York.

Chase, A. 1977. *The Legacy of Malthus: The Social Costs of the New Scientific Racism*. New York.

Choucri, N. 1974. *Population Dynamics and International Violence*. Lexington, Mass.

Choussy, F. 1924. *El algodón en El Salvador*. San Salvador.

————. 1950. *Economía de la industria cafetalera*. Reprinted 1972 by Grupo Técnico Para la Renegociación del Convenio Internacional de Café. San Salvador.

Clark, C. 1967. *Population Growth and Land Use*. New York.

Clarke, J. I. 1973. Population pressure on resources: The problem of evaluation. In B. Benjamin et al., eds., *Resources and Population*, pp. 109–17. New York.

Cohen, M. N. 1977. *The Food Crisis in Prehistory: Overpopulation and the Origins of Agriculture*. New Haven, Conn.

Colindres, E. 1976. La tenencia de la tierra en El Salvador. *Estudios Centroamericanos*. 31 (335/36): 463–72.

Collier, B. D., et al. 1973. *Dynamic Ecology*. Englewood Cliffs, N.J.

Comisión Económica Para América Latina. 1970. *Características generales de la utilización y distribución de la tierra en Honduras*. Mexico City.

————. 1971. *El Salvador: Características generales de la utilización y distribución de la tierra*. Mexico City.

————. 1973. *Tenencia de la tierra y desarrollo rural en Centroamérica*. San José, Costa Rica.

Commoner, B. 1975. How poverty breeds overpopulation (and not the other way around). *Ramparts* 13 (10): 21ff.

Consejo Nacional de Planificación. 1969. *Cuantificación y análisis de la población salvadoreña expulsada de Honduras.* Documento DT/785. San Salvador.

Consejo Superior de Planificación Económica. 1974. *Evaluación espacial del uso actual y potencial de la tierra de Honduras.* Tegucigalpa.

Cooperativa Algodonera Salvadoreña. 1972. *Memoria.* San Salvador.

Cortez y Larraz, P. 1921 (1770). Descripción geográfico-moral de la Provincia de San Salvador. In El Salvador, Ministerio de Relaciones Exteriores y Instrucción Pública, *Colección de documentos importantes relativos a la República de El Salvador.* San Salvador.

Croat, T. B. 1972. The role of overpopulation and agricultural methods in the destruction of tropical ecosystems. *Bioscience* 22: 465–67.

Cuenca, A. 1962. *El Salvador: Una democracia cafetalera.* Mexico City.

Daugherty, H. E. 1969. Man-induced ecologic change in El Salvador. Ph.D. dissertation, University of California, Los Angeles.

———. 1972. The impact of man on the zoogeography of El Salvador. *Biological Conservation* 4 (4): 273–78.

———. 1973a. *Conservación ambiental en El Salvador: Recomendaciones para un programa de acción nacional.* San Salvador.

———. 1973b. The conflict between accelerating economic demands and regional ecologic stability in coastal El Salvador. In A. D. Hill, ed., *Latin American Development Issues*, pp. 1–13. East Lansing, Mich.

Davis, J. 1973. *Land and Family in Pisticci.* New York.

de Paredes, Q., et al. 1969. Características de la población migrante. In Departamento de Ciencias Sociales, Facultad de Humanidades, Universidad de El Salvador, *Contribución al estudio del conflicto hondureño-salvadoreño.* San Salvador.

Del Cid, J. R. 1975. Reforma agraria y capitalismo dependiente: Análisis sociológico del decreto ley #170 y la ley de reforma agraria en Honduras. Thesis, Departamento de Sociología, Universidad de Costa Rica, San José.

Denevan, W. M. 1976. *The Native Population of the Americas in 1492.* Madison, Wis.

Durham, W. H. 1976a. Resource competition and human aggression, Part 1: A review of primitive war. *Quarterly Review of Biology* 51: 385–415.

———. 1976b. The adaptive significance of cultural behavior. *Human Ecology* 4 (2): 89–121.

———. 1979. Toward a coevolutionary theory of human biology and culture. In W. Irons and N. Chagnon, eds., *Evolutionary Biology and Human Social Behavior*, North Scituate, Mass.

Eckholm, E. P. 1976. *Losing Ground.* New York.

Economic Commission on Latin America. 1961. *The Economic Development of Honduras.* New York.

Ehrlich, P. R. 1968. *The Population Bomb.* New York.

————. 1970. Population control or Hobson's choice. In I. R. Taylor, ed., *The Optimum Population for Britain*, pp. 151–62. London.

Ehrlich, P. R., and A. H. Ehrlich. 1972. *Population, Resources, Environment: Issues in Human Ecology.* San Francisco, Calif.

————. 1976. The world food problem: No room for complacency. *Social Science Quarterly* 57: 375–82.

Ehrlich, P. R., A. H. Ehrlich, and J. P. Holdren. 1977. *Ecoscience: Population, Resources and Environment.* San Francisco, Calif.

Eisenberg, R. M. 1966. The regulation of density in a natural population of the pond snail, *Lymnaea elodes. Ecology* 47: 889–94.

El Salvador, *see* Salvador.

Elam, R. V. 1968. Appeal to arms: The army and politics in El Salvador, 1931–1964. Ph.D. dissertation, University of New Mexico, Albuquerque.

Emlen, J. M. 1973. *Ecology: An Evolutionary Approach.* Reading, Mass.

Environmental Fund. 1976. Statement on the real crisis behind the food crisis. *Smithsonian* 6 (12): 28–29.

Euceda Gómez, A. 1968. El problema agrario, el problema urbano y la integración de la ciudad y el campo de Honduras. *Economía Política* 17: 19–65.

Fagan, S. I. 1970. *Central American Economic Integration: The Politics of Unequal Benefits.* Research Series no. 15, Institute of International Studies, University of California. Berkeley.

Feder, E. 1971. *The Rape of the Peasantry: Latin America's Landholding System.* Garden City, N.Y.

Flemion, P. F. 1972. *Historical Dictionary of El Salvador.* Metuchen, N.J.

Fonck, C. O. 1972. *Modernity and Public Policies in the Context of the Peasant Sector: Honduras as a Case Study.* Dissertation Series no. 32, Latin American Studies Program, Cornell University. Ithaca, N.Y.

Fox, D. J., and K. E. Guire. 1976. *Documentation for MIDAS.* Ann Arbor, Mich. 3d ed.

Fox, R. W., and J. W. Huguet. 1977. *Population and Urban Trends in Central America and Panama.* Washington, D.C.

Freeman, J. M. 1977. *Scarcity and Opportunity in an Indian Village.* Menlo Park, Calif.

Friedrich, P. 1970. *Agrarian Revolt in a Mexican Village.* Englewood Cliffs, N.J.

Fuentes Rivera, L. 1971. El conflicto Honduras-El Salvador: Aspectos políticos, sociales y económicos. In Carías and Slutzky, cited above, pp. 303–38.

Gause, G. F. 1934. *The Struggle for Existence.* New York.

Gavan, J. D., and J. A. Dixon. 1975. India: A perspective on the food situation. *Science* 183: 541–49.

Geisert, H. L. 1959. *Population Problems in Mexico and Central America.* Washington, D.C.

————. 1963. *Population Growth and International Migration.* Washington, D.C.

George, S. 1977. *How the Other Half Dies: The Real Reasons for World Hunger.* Montclair, N.J.

Gerstein, J. A. 1971. Conflicto Honduras-Salvador. *Foro Internacional* 11: 552–69.

Gómez, F., et al. 1956. Mortality in second and third degree malnutrition. *Journal of Tropical Pediatrics* 2: 77.

Gómez, M. A. 1974. *El movimiento campesino y la reforma agraria en Honduras.* Tegucigalpa.

González, A. 1967. Some effects of population growth on Latin America's economy. *Journal of Inter-American Studies* 9: 22–42.

Griffin, K. 1976. *Land Concentration and Rural Poverty.* New York.

Grunwald, J., and P. Musgrove. 1970. *Natural Resources in Latin American Development.* Baltimore, Md.

Guerrero, F. T. 1969. *Position of El Salvador Before the Inter-American Commission on Human Rights.* San Salvador.

Gutiérrez y Ulloa, A. 1807. *Estado general de la Provincia de El Salvador.* San Salvador. Reprinted 1962.

Hankins, F. H. 1940. Pressures of population as a cause of war. *Annals of the American Academy of Political and Social Science* 198: 101–8.

Hardin, C. M. 1969. *Overcoming World Hunger.* Englewood Cliffs, N.J.

Hardin, G. 1974a. Living on a lifeboat. *Bioscience* 24 (10): 561–68.

———. 1974b. Lifeboat ethics. The case against helping the poor. *Psychology Today,* September: 38ff.

———. 1977. *The Limits of Altruism: An Ecologist's View of Survival.* Bloomington, Ind.

Harner, M. J. 1970. Population pressure and the social evolution of agriculturalists. *Southwestern Journal of Anthropology* 26: 67–86.

Hart, J. F. 1970. The adjustment of rural populations to diminishing land resources. In Zelinsky et al., cited below, pp. 95–99.

Hartley, S. F. 1972. *Population Quantity Versus Quality: A Sociological Examination of the Causes and Consequences of the Population Explosion.* Englewood Cliffs, N.J.

Harvey, D. 1974. Population, resources, and the ideology of science. *Economic Geography* 50: 256–77.

Heer, D., and D. O. Smith. 1967. Mortality level and desired family size. Paper contributed to the Sydney Conference of the International Union for the Scientific Study of Population.

Hirsch, L. 1966. The littoral highway in El Salvador. In G. W. Wilson et al., eds., *The Impact of Highway Investment on Development,* pp. 87–126. Washington, D.C.

Honduras. Dirección General de Estadística y Censos. 1932. *Resumen del censo general de población levantado el 29 de junio de 1930.* Tegucigalpa.

———. 1952. *Resumen general del censo de población levantado el 18 de junio de 1950.* Tegucigalpa.

———. 1954. *Primer censo agropecuario.* San Salvador.

———. 1964a. *Censo nacional de Honduras, 1961.* Tegucigalpa.

―――. 1964b. *Características económicas de la población.* Tegucigalpa.

―――. 1964c. *División político-territorial.* Tegucigalpa.

―――. 1967. Número y superficie de las fincas, existencia de ganado, según tamaño y tenencia de las fincas por departamento y municipio (cifras preliminares). Tegucigalpa. Mimeo.

―――. 1968. *Segundo censo nacional agropecuario, 1965–1966.* Tegucigalpa.

―――. 1975. *Cifras preliminares del tercer censo nacional agropecuario.* Tegucigalpa.

―――. 1977. *Anuario estadístico, 1975.* Tegucigalpa.

Hutchinson, E. P. 1967. *The Population Debate.* Boston, Mass.

Indicadores económicos y sociales. 1963–76. Consejo Nacional de Planificación. San Salvador. (For respective years.)

Instituto Geográfico Nacional. 1973. *Diccionario geográfico de El Salvador,* Vol. 2. San Salvador.

Instituto de Investigaciones Económicas y Sociales. 1961a. *Tenencia de la tierra y condiciones del trabajo agrícola.* Tegucigalpa.

―――. 1961b. *Tierras y colonización.* Monografía no. 2, Universidad Nacional Autónoma de Honduras. Tegucigalpa.

―――. 1964. *Estudio económico de la aldea de Flores.* Tegucigalpa.

Instituto Nacional Agrario. 1968–69. *Memorias.* Tegucigalpa.

―――. 1976. ¿Qué es la reforma agraria hondureña? Tegucigalpa.

Instituto de Nutrición de Centro América y Panama. 1969. *Evaluación nutricional de la población de Centroamérica y Panamá.* Guatemala City.

Jiménez, E. E. 1974. *La guerra no fue de fútbol.* Havana, Cuba.

Johannessen, C. L. 1963. *Savannas of Interior Honduras.* Ibero-Americana 46. Berkeley, Calif.

Johnson, A. W. 1971. *Sharecroppers of the Sertão.* Stanford, Calif.

Jonas, S. 1973. Design and manipulation of the Central American Common Market. *NACLA's Latin America and Empire Report* 7 (5): 3–21.

Kaplan, B. A., ed. 1976. *Anthropological Studies of Human Fertility.* Detroit.

Kelly, R. C. 1968. Demographic pressure and descent group structure in the New Guinea highlands. *Oceania* 39: 36–63.

Kemp, G. 1970. Arms traffic and Third World countries. *International Conciliation* 577: 1–77.

Kepner, C. D., and J. H. Soothill. 1935. *The Banana Empire: A Case Study of Economic Imperialism.* New York.

Kessinger, T. G. 1974. *Vilyatpur 1848–1968: Social and Economic Change in a North Indian Village.* Berkeley, Calif.

Kocher, J. E. 1973. *Rural Development, Income Distribution and Fertility Decline.* Occasional paper of the Population Council. New York.

Kosinski, L., and R. M. Prothero. 1970. Migrations and population pressures on resources. In Zelinsky et al., cited below, pp. 251–58.

Laínez, V., and V. Meza. 1973. El enclave bananero en la historia de Honduras. *Estudios Sociales Centroamericanos* 2 (5): 119–56.

Lappé, F. M., and J. Collins. 1977. *Food First: Beyond the Myth of Scarcity.* Boston, Mass.

Larde y Larín, J. 1957. *El Salvador: Historia de sus pueblos, villas y ciudades.* San Salvador.

Lipton, M. 1977. *Why Poor People Stay Poor.* Cambridge, Mass.

Loenholdt, F. 1953. *The Agricultural Economy of El Salvador.* San Salvador.

López, L. 1858. *Estadística general de la República de El Salvador.* San Salvador.

Love, T. T. 1977. Ecological niche theory in sociocultural anthropology: A conceptual framework and an application. *American Ethnologist* 4 (1): 27–41.

Lovo Castelar, L. 1967. La distribución y tenencia de la tierra en El Salvador. *La Universidad* 92 (4): 107–15.

Luna, D. A. 1971. *Manual de historia económica de El Salvador.* San Salvador.

MacArthur, R. H. 1972. *Geographical Ecology: Patterns in the Distribution of Species.* New York.

MacFarlane, A. 1976. *Resources and Population: A Study of the Gurungs of Nepal.* Cambridge, Eng.

MacLeod, M. 1973. *Spanish Central America: A Socioeconomic History, 1520–1720.* Berkeley, Calif.

Malthus, T. R. 1970 (1798). *An Essay on the Principle of Population.* Baltimore, Md.

Mamdani, M. 1972. *The Myth of Population Control.* New York.

Márquez, J., et al. 1950. *Estudio sobre la economía de Honduras.* Tegucigalpa.

Marroquín, A. D. 1962. *San Pedro Nonualco: Investigación sociológica.* San Salvador.

———. 1964. *Apreciación sociológica de la independencia salvadoreña.* San Salvador.

———. 1965. Cambios en la agricultura y sus repercusiones sociales. *Revista Salvadoreña de Ciencias Sociales* 1 (1): 109–51.

———. 1974. *Panchimalco.* San Salvador. 2d ed.

Martín-Baró, I. 1977. Social attitudes and group conflict in El Salvador. M.A. thesis, Master's Program in Social Science, University of Chicago.

Martínez Cuestras, A. 1965. *La agricultura de los productos de subsistencia en El Salvador.* San Salvador.

Mass, B. 1976. *Population Target: The Political Economy of Population Control in Latin America.* Brompton, Ontario.

Maturana Medina, S. 1962. *Las relaciones entre la tenencia de la tierra y la eficiencia del uso de los recursos agrícolas en Centro América.* San Pedro de Montes de Oca, Mexico.

May, D. A., and D. M. Heer. 1968. Son survivorship, motivation and family size in India: A computer simulation. *Population Studies* 22 (2): 199–210.

May, J. M., and D. L. McClellan. 1972. *The Ecology of Malnutrition in Mexico and Central America.* New York.

Mayer, J. 1976. The dimensions of human hunger. *Scientific American* 235 (3): 40–49.

Mayorga Quirós, R. 1974. La presión demográfica en El Salvador, las trampas neomalthusianas y la teoría de la reventazón. *Estudios Centroamericanos* 29 (310/11): 603–38.

Meadows, D. H., et al. 1972. *The Limits to Growth.* New York.

Meek, R. L. 1971. *Marx and Engels on the Population Bomb.* Berkeley, Calif.

Mellor, J. W. 1976. *The New Economics of Growth.* Ithaca, N.Y.

Menjívar, R. 1962. *Formas de tenencia de la tierra y algunos otros aspectos de la actividad agropecuaria.* Monografía no. 1, Instituto de Estudios Económicos, Universidad de El Salvador. San Salvador.

Meza, V., and H. López. 1973. Las inversiones extranjeras en Honduras antes del Mercado Común Centroamericano. *Economía Política* 6: 47–80.

Micklin, M., ed. 1973. *Population, Environment and Social Organization: Current Issues in Human Ecology.* Hillsdale, Ill.

Milne, A. 1961. Definition of competition among animals. *Symposium of the Society of Experimental Biology* 15: 40–61.

Molina Chocano, G. 1975a. Estructura productiva e historia demográfica. *Economía Política* 10: 44–65.

———. 1975b. Población, estructura productiva y migraciones internos en Honduras (1950–1960). *Estudios Sociales Centroamericanos* 12: 9–39.

Monteforte Toledo, M. 1972. *Centro América: Subdesarollo y dependencia.* Mexico City.

Mundigo, A. I. 1972. *Elites, Economic Development and Population in Honduras.* Dissertation Series no. 34, Latin America Studies Program, Cornell University. Ithaca, N.Y.

Murdoch, W. W., and A. Oaten. 1975. Population and food: Metaphors and the reality. *Bioscience* 25 (9): 561–67.

Murga Frassinetti, A. 1973. Estructura agraria y latifundio: El caso de Honduras. *Economía Política* 5: 31–63.

Nathan, R. R., and Associates. 1969. *Agricultural Sectoral Analysis for El Salvador.* San Salvador.

National Academy of Sciences. 1971. *Rapid Population Growth: Consequences and Policy Implications.* Baltimore, Md.

Ophuls, W. 1977. *Ecology and the Politics of Scarcity.* San Francisco, Calif.

Organization of American States. 1963. *Informe oficial de la misión 105 de asistencia técnica directa a Honduras sobre reforma agraria y desarollo agrícola.* Washington, D.C.

———. 1974. *El Salvador: Zonificación agrícola.* Washington, D.C.

Overbeek, J. 1974. *History of Population Theories.* Rotterdam.

———. 1976. *The Population Challenge.* Westport, Conn.

Owen, D. F. 1976. Human inequality: An ecologist's point of view. *Oikos* 27: 2–8.

Parsons, J. J. 1976. Forest to pasture: Development or destruction? *Revista de Biología Tropical* 24 (supl. 1): 121–38.

Parsons, K. H. 1976. *Agrarian Reform in Southern Honduras.* Research Paper no. 67, Land Tenure Center, University of Wisconsin. Madison.

Pérez Brignoli, H. 1973a. Economía y sociedad en Honduras durante el siglo XIX. *Estudios Sociales Centroamericanos* 11 (6): 51–82.

198   *Bibliography*

————. 1973b. La reforma liberal en Honduras. In *Cuadernos de Ciencias Sociales #2.* Tegucigalpa.

Plath, C. U. 1967. *Uso potencial de la tierra en Honduras,* Part 5. Rome.

Ponce, J. M. 1974. *Antecedentes y perspectivas de la reforma agraria en Honduras.* Tegucigalpa.

Population Reference Bureau. 1969. The Soccer War. *Population Bulletin* 25 (6): 134.

Posas Amador, M. 1976. El movimiento obrero hondureño: La huelga de 1954 y sus consecuencias. *Estudios Sociales Centroamericanos* 15: 93–127.

Programa de Capacitación Campesina para la Reforma Agraria. 1975. *Estrategia de desarrollo y reforma agraria: La opción hondureña.* Tegucigalpa.

Puffer, R. R., and C. V. Serrano. 1973. *Patterns of Mortality in Childhood.* Washington, D.C.

Ratcliffe, J. 1978. Social justice and the demographic transition: Lessons from India's Kerala state. *International Journal of Health Services,* 8 (1): 123–44.

Rawson, I. G., and V. Valverde. 1976. The etiology of malnutrition among preschool children in rural Costa Rica. *Environmental Child Health* 22: 12–17.

Raynolds, D. R. 1967. *Rapid Development in Small Economies: The Example of El Salvador.* New York.

Reutlinger, S., and M. Selowsky. 1976. *Malnutrition and Poverty.* Baltimore, Md.

Revelle, R. 1966. Population and food supplies: The edge of the knife. *Proceedings of the National Academy of Science* 56 (2): 328–51.

Reyes, R. 1888. *Apuntamientos estadísticos sobre la República del Salvador.* San Salvador.

Rich, W. 1973. *Smaller Families Through Social and Economic Progress.* Washington, D.C.

Richerson, P. J. 1977. Ecology and human ecology: A comparison of theories in the biological and social sciences. *American Ethnologist* 4 (1): 1–26.

Richter, E. 1974. Consideraciones sobre el factor de superpoblación en el conflicto entre El Salvador y Honduras. Paper presented at the Encuentro de Ciudadanos Centroamericanas para Examinar los Problemas Relativos al Conflicto Entre Honduras y El Salvador. San José, Costa Rica.

Royer, D. K. 1966. Economic development of El Salvador, 1945–1965. Ph.D. dissertation, University of Florida.

Russell, E. B. 1964. Population pressure and war. In S. Mudd, ed, *The Population Crisis and the Use of World Resources,* pp. 1–5. Bloomington, Ind.

Sadleir, R. M. F. S. 1972. Environmental effects. In C. R. Austin and R. V. Short, eds., *Reproduction in Mammals,* Vol. 4: *Reproductive Patterns,* pp. 69–93. Cambridge, Eng.

Sahlins, M. 1972. *Stone Age Economics.* Chicago.

Salvador, El. Asamblea Legislativa. 1970. *Memoria del primer congreso nacional de reforma agraria.* San Salvador.

————. Dirección General de Estadística y Censos. 1942. *Población de la República de El Salvador: Censo de primer mayo de 1930.* San Salvador.

———. 1953. *Segundo censo de la población.* San Salvador.

———. 1954. *Censo agropecuario, Octubre-Diciembre de 1950.* San Salvador.

———. 1955. *Atlas censal de El Salvador.* San Salvador.

———. 1965. *Tercer censo nacional de población, 1961.* San Salvador.

———. 1967. *Segundo censo agropecuario, 1961.* San Salvador.

———. 1974a. *Cuarto censo nacional de población, 1971,* Vol. 1. San Salvador.

———. 1974b. *Tercer censo nacional agropecuario,* Vol. 1. San Salvador.

———. 1974c. *Tercer censo nacional de vivienda, 1971.* San Salvador.

———. 1975. *Tercer censo nacional agropecuario,* Vol. 2. San Salvador.

———. 1977. *Cuarto censo nacional de población, 1971,* Vol. 2. San Salvador.

———. Ministerio de Agricultura y Ganadería. 1963–70. *Anuario de prognósticos* (for respective years). San Salvador.

———. 1970–75. *Anuario de estadísticas agropecuarias* (for respective years). San Salvador.

———. 1973. *Estudio para la fijación del salario minimo, sector agropecuario 1973.* San Salvador.

———. 1977. *Plan de desarrollo agropecuario, 1978-1982.* San Salvador.

[Other official and semiofficial publications are listed by title or by institutional name.]

Santos De Morais, C. 1975. The role of the campesino sector in the Honduran agrarian reform. *Land Tenure Center Newsletter* (University of Wisconsin) 47: 16–22.

Satterthwaite, R. 1971. Campesino agriculture and hacienda modernization in coastal El Salvador: 1949 to 1969. Ph.D. dissertation, University of Wisconsin. Madison.

Secretaria de Comunicación Social del Arzobispado de San Salvador. 1978. Los sucesos de San Pedro Perulapán. *Estudios Centramericanos,* 33 (354): 223–47.

Seligson, M. A. 1974. The peasant and agrarian capitalism in Costa Rica. Ph.D. dissertation, University of Pittsburgh.

———. 1975. *Agrarian Capitalism and the Transformation of Peasant Society: Coffee in Costa Rica.* Special Studies Series, State University of New York. Buffalo.

Sermeño Lima, J. A. 1974. El Salvador, 1985–2000: Población y recursos naturales. *Estudios Sociales Centroamericanos* 3 (9): 207–54.

Severin, T. 1969. Pressure in El Salvador. *Geographical Magazine* 41: 278–86.

Shaw, R. P. 1976. *Land Tenure and the Rural Exodus in Chile, Colombia, Costa Rica, and Peru.* Gainesville, Fla.

Simkins, P. D. 1970. Migration as a response to population pressure: The case of the Philippines. In Zelinsky et al., cited below, pp. 259–67.

Skinner, G. W. 1971. Chinese peasants and the closed community: An open and shut case. *Comparative Studies in Society and History* 13: 270–81.

Smith, R. A. 1965. El Salvador diversifies export crops but lags in food production. *Foreign Agriculture,* Oct. 4: 3–5.

Smith, T. L. 1945. Notes on population and rural social organization in El Salvador. *Rural Sociology* 10: 359–79.

————. 1976. *The Race Between Population and Food Supply in Latin America.* Albuquerque, N. Mex.

Spooner, B., ed. 1972. *Population Growth: Anthropological Implications.* Cambridge, Mass.

Stares, R. C. 1971. Estudio de ingresos y gastos familiares en la zona sur de Honduras. Report presented to the prelacy of Choluteca, Honduras.

————. 1972. La economía campesina en la zona sur de Honduras, 1950–1970: Su desarollo y perspectivas para el futuro. Report presented to the prefecture of Choluteca, Honduras.

Stokes, W. S. 1947. The land laws of Honduras. *Agricultural History* 21: 148–54.

Stycos, J. M. 1974. Latin American overpopulation shoves thousands to margin of life. *Smithsonian* 5 (1): 74–81.

Stys, W. 1957a. The influence of economic conditions on the fertility of peasant women. *Population Studies* 11 (2): 136–48.

————. 1957b. *Wspolzaleznosc Rozwoju Rodziny Chlopskiej i Jej Gospodarstwa.* (Correlation between the size of peasant families and the size of their holdings.) Warsaw.

Teller, C. H. 1972. Internal Migration, Socio-Economic Status and Health: Access to Medical Care in a Honduran City. Dissertation Series no. 41, Latin American Studies Program, Cornell University. Ithaca, N.Y.

Thomas, R. N. 1971. Internal migration in Latin America: An analysis of recent literature. In B. Lentnek et al., *Geographic Research on Latin America: Benchmark 1970*, pp. 104–18. Muncie, Ind.

————. 1975. Migrant paths to Tegucigalpa and San Pedro Sula, Honduras: The role of accessibility. *Social and Economic Studies* 24: 445–57.

Toña Velasco, C. 1974. Tenencia y uso de la tierra, su incidencia en la utilización de mano de obra agrícola. Caso: Ahuachapán, El Salvador. Thesis, Universidad Centroamericana José Simeón Cañas, San Salvador.

Torres, A. 1961. Tierras y colonización, régimen de tenencia de la tierra y condiciónes de trabajo agricola en El Salvador. Monografía no. 2, Instituto de Estudios Económicos, Universidad de El Salvador. San Salvador.

————. 1962. More from this land: Agrarian reform in El Salvador. *Americas* 14 (8): 6–12.

Torres-Rivas, E. 1971. Familia y juventud en El Salvador. In A. Gurrieri et al., eds., *Estudios sobre la juventud marginal latinoamericana*, pp. 195–281. Mexico City.

United Nations. 1954. *The Population of Central America Including Mexico, 1950–1980.* New York.

United States House of Representatives Committee on International Relations. 1977 (July 21 and 29). *Religious Persecution in El Salvador.* Washington, D.C.

Vallejo, A. R. 1888. *Censo general de la República de Honduras, 1887.* Tegucigalpa.

Valverde, V., et al. 1977. Relationship between family land availability and nutritional status. *Ecology of Food and Nutrition* 6: 1–7.

Vandermeer, J. H. 1969. The competitive structure of communities: An experimental approach with Protozoa. *Ecology* 50: 362–71.

———. 1976. Hardin's lifeboat adrift. *Science for the People*, Jan.: 16–19.

———. 1977. Ecological determinism. In Ann Arbor Science for the People Editorial Collective, eds., *Biology as a Social Weapon*, pp. 108–122. Minneapolis.

Vayda, A. P., and R. A. Rappaport. 1968. Ecology, cultural and noncultural. In J. A. Clifton, ed., *Introduction to Cultural Anthropology*, pp. 477–97. Boston.

Vermeer, D. E. 1970. Population pressure and crop rotational changes among the Tiv of Nigeria. *Annals of the Association of American Geographers* 66 (2): 299–314.

Verner, J. G. 1975. Legislative attitude toward overpopulation: The case of El Salvador. *Journal of Developing Areas* 10 (1): 61–76.

Vieytez, A. 1969. La emigración salvadoreña a Honduras. *Estudios Centroamericanos* 24 (254/55): 399–406.

Villanueva, B. 1968a. *The Role of Institutional Innovations in the Economic Development of Honduras.* Research Paper No. 34, Land Tenure Center, University of Wisconsin. Madison.

———. 1968b. Institutional innovation and economic development: Honduras, a case study. Ph.D. dissertation, University of Wisconsin. Madison.

Vogt, W. 1946. *The Population of El Salvador and Its Natural Resources.* Washington, D.C.

———. 1948. *Road to Survival.* New York.

———, ed. 1965. *Human Conservation in Central America.* Washington, D.C.

Waterston, A. 1949. *Report on the Economy of El Salvador.* Economic Department International Bank for Reconstruction and Development. Washington, D.C.

Weiner, J. S., and J. A. Lourie, 1969. *Human Biology: A Guide to Field Methods.* Oxford, Eng.

Welton, R. S. 1967. El Salvador plans crop diversification to spur its economy. *Foreign Agriculture* 5 (32): 5–6.

West, R. C., and J. P. Augelli. 1976. *Middle America: Its Lands and Peoples.* Englewood Cliffs, N.J. 2d ed.

White, A. 1973. *El Salvador.* New York.

White, B. 1975. The economic importance of children in a Javanese village. In M. Nag, ed., *Population and Social Organization*, pp. 127–46. Chicago.

White, R. A. 1972. The adult education program of Acción Cultural Popular Hondureña. Department of Anthropology and Sociology, University of Missouri. St. Louis.

———. 1977. Structural factors in rural development: The church and the peasant in Honduras. Ph.D. dissertation, Cornell University.

Wilbur, C. K. 1977. The role of population in Western economic thought. Working Paper no. A1, Department of Economics, University of Notre Dame.

Wilbur, H. M. 1972. Competition, predation, and the structure of the *Ambystoma-Rana sylvatica* community. *Ecology* 53 (1): 1–21.

Williams, L. S. 1971. The overpopulation concept and the Latin Americanist geographer. In B. Lentnek et al., *Geographic Research on Latin America: Benchmark 1970*, pp. 119–23. Muncie, Ind.

Williamson, R. C. 1959. Population dynamics in El Salvador. *Sociology and Social Research* 43 (6): 421–26.

Wilson, E. A. 1970. The crisis of national integration in El Salvador, 1919–1935. Ph.D. dissertation, Stanford University.

Wilson, E. C., and W. H. Bossert. 1971. *A Primer of Population Biology.* Stamford, Conn.

Wise, D. 1974. The role of food supply in the population dynamics of the spider *Linyphia marginata.* Ph.D. dissertation, University of Michigan. Ann Arbor.

Wolf, E. 1955. Types of Latin American peasantry: A preliminary discussion. *American Anthropologist* 57: 452–71.

Wortman, S. 1976. Food and agriculture. *Scientific American* 235 (3): 31–39.

Young, G. L. 1974. Human ecology as an interdisciplinary concept: A critical inquiry. In A. Macfayden, ed., *Advances in Ecological Research*, Vol. 8, pp. 1–105. New York.

Zamora, R. 1976. ¿Seguro de vida o despojo? Análisis político de la transformación agraria. *Estudios Centroamericanos*, 31 (335/36): 511–34.

Zelinsky, W. 1966. The geographer and his crowding world: Cautionary notes toward the study of population pressure in the "developing lands." *Revista Geográfica* 64: 7–28.

Zelinsky, W., L. A. Kosinski, and R. M. Prothero. 1970. *Geography and a Crowding World: A Symposium on Population Pressures upon Physical and Social Resources in the Developing Lands.* New York.

Zobel, D. C. 1967. *Estudio post-censal: Segundo censo nacional agropecuario de Honduras.* Tegucigalpa.

Index

Index